Classical Greek Prose
A Basic Vocabulary

A classified list of 1500 of the commonest words

MALCOLM CAMPBELL

Bristol Classical Press

This impression 2003
This edition published in 1998 by
Bristol Classical Press
an imprint of
Gerald Duckworth & Co. Ltd.
90-93 Cowcross Street, London EC1M 6BF
Tel: 020 7490 7300
Fax: 020 7490 0080
inquiries@duckworth-publishers.co.uk
www.ducknet.co.uk

© 1998 by Malcolm Campbell

A catalogue record for this book is available
from the British Library

ISBN 1 85399 559 2

CONTENTS

PREFACE

My thanks to John Betts for giving this project a home; to Jean Scott and Graham Douglas at Bristol Classical Press for advice on book-production; to my wife Dorothy and son Richard for their support; to a number of students in the Greek classes at St Andrews for offering various helpful comments; and to my colleague Dr Niall Livingstone for providing me with detailed annotations on the penultimate draft and showing me ways of making it more user-friendly.

St Andrews, January 1998   M.C.

INTRODUCTION

This book provides a basic vocabulary of Classical Attic Prose. The aim is that students drilled in it should be able to read texts without constant recourse to a dictionary, and that tutors can use it as a reference-point in determining what help should be provided in unseen translation exercises. It was compiled by assembling all words in common use and adding to them a body of words recurrent in a selection of twelve prose works (by Thucydides, Plato and orators) currently marketed as 'set texts', until the point was reached where it was felt that all but the most abstruse or technical passages could be read with relative comfort.

Note the following points:
1 The standard format of vocabulary books, that of one single undifferentiated string of words, has not been adopted (though an alphabetical index is provided). Instead, words are listed according to type.
2 On the other hand, the conventional listing by columns has been retained to facilitate rapid self-testing. It is highly desirable however that more information is absorbed about some very important basic words than can be conveyed by such a format. For this reason, 100 of the 1500 words, identified by the symbol *, are dealt with at greater length in a Supplement (arranged alphabetically). Here the opportunity is taken to incorporate some illustrations of Greek idiom.
3 Not every meaning is offered for every word, only the commonest.
4 It is worth taking the time to build up a picture of word-families: under many entries cognates are given with numerical cross-references to enable the user to track down any word in the collection instantly. The overall numeration will enable tutors to set blocks drawn from different parts of speech for the purposes of classroom testing, whether written or oral.
5 Not included here : most numerals; corresponding μή-forms for negative words beginning with οὐ-

ABBREVIATIONS

abs.:	absolute(ly)	n.:	noun
acc.:	accusative	neg.:	negative
adj.:	adjective	neut.:	neuter
adv.:	adverb or adverbial(ly)	opp.:	opposite
aor.:	aorist	optat.:	optative
cf.:	compare	part.:	participle
com.:	comparative	pass.:	passive
conj.:	conjunction	perf.:	perfect
cpd:	compound	plur.:	plural
ctr.:	contrast	postp.:	postpositive
dat.:	dative	prep.:	preposition
fem.:	feminine	pres.:	present
foreg.:	foregoing	s.:	sub
freq.:	frequent(ly)	sc.:	scilicet
fut.:	future	sing.:	singular
gen.:	genitive	sts:	sometimes
imp.:	imperative	subjv.:	subjunctive
impers.:	impersonal(ly)	sup.:	superlative
indic.:	indicative	Supp.:	Supplement
inf.:	infinitive	v.:	vide
intrans.:	intransitive(ly)	vb:	verb
masc.:	masculine	w.:	with

Entries marked *: consult the Supplement for further elucidation

I. NOUNS

A. MASCULINE NOUNS

1.a -ΑΣ, genitive -ΟΥ

1 νεανίας — *young man, youth*, sts with ref. to headstrong, unruly, irresponsible conduct
• Cf. n. νεανίσκος[76], adj. νέος[590]

1.b -ΗΣ, genitive -ΟΥ

2 δεσπότης — household *master*, esp. in relation to slaves; *absolute ruler*

3 δικαστής — *juror*, ὦ ἄνδρες -αί 'gentlemen of the jury'
• Cf. n. δικαστήριον[394], vb δικάζειν[912]

4 ἐπιστάτης — *overseer, supervisor, director*
• Cf. vb ἐφ-ιστάναι/ -ίστασθαι[1351]

5 ἐραστής — *lover; ardent admirer, devotee*
• Cf. vb ἐρᾶν[1152], n. ἔρως[142]

6 εὐεργέτης — *benefactor*
• Cf. n. εὐεργεσία[202], vb εὐεργετεῖν[1230]

7 θεατής — *spectator*, plur. *audience*
• Cf. n. θέατρον[398], vb θεᾶσθαι[1173]

8 ἰδιώτης — *(private) individual*, often as opposed to polis or to holder of public office; *layman* as opposed to specialist
• Cf. adj. ἴδιος[576]

9 ἱκέτης — *suppliant*
• Cf. vb ἱκετεύειν[950]

10 κλέπτης — *thief, burglar*
• Cf. vb κλέπτειν[970], n. κλοπή[299]

11 κυβερνήτης — *steersman, pilot*

12 λῃστής — *robber, pirate*
• Cf. vb λῄζεσθαι[1112]

13 ναύτης — *sailor*, plur. ship's *crew*
• Cf. n. ναῦς[377], ναυτικόν[403]

14 νομοθέτης — *lawgiver, legislator*
• Cf. n. νόμος[78], vb τιθέναι[1370]

¹⁵ οἰκέτης

house-slave, menial
• Cf. n. οἶκος⁸⁰

¹⁶ ὁπλίτης

In plur. *hoplites, (heavy-armed) infantry*
• Cf. n. ὅπλα⁴⁰⁶, τά, vb ὁπλίζειν¹⁰⁰³

¹⁷ ποιητής

maker, composer, author, esp. poet
• Cf. vb ποιεῖν¹²⁶⁶, n. ποίημα⁴⁶⁶, ποίησις³⁵⁴

¹⁸ πολίτης

citizen, fellow-citizen
• Cf. n. πόλις³⁵⁵, πολιτεία²³⁷,
vb πολιτεύεσθαι¹¹²⁶, adj. πολιτικός⁵²⁸

¹⁹ προδότης

betrayer, traitor
• Cf. vb προ-διδόναι¹³⁶⁷, n. προδοσία²³⁹

²⁰ σοφιστής

skilled practitioner of an art; *sophist*
• Cf. n. σοφία²⁴³, adj. σοφός⁵³²

²¹ στρατιώτης

member of a στρατιά, *soldier*, sts *sailor*
• Cf. n. στρατιά²⁴⁵, vb στρατεύεσθαι¹¹³¹

²² συκοφάντης

professional informer/ prosecutor
• Cf. vb συκοφαντεῖν¹²⁷⁶

²³ τοξότης

bowman, archer
• Cf. n. τόξον⁴¹⁶

²⁴ ὑπηρέτης

servant, attendant, underling, subordinate
• Cf. vb ὑπηρετεῖν¹²⁸¹

2.a/1 -ΟΣ, genitive -ΟΥ

²⁵ ἄγγελος

messenger
• Cf. n. ἀγγελία¹⁶⁵, vb ἀγγέλλειν⁸⁶⁶

²⁶ ἀγρός

field; country as opposed to town
• Cf. adj. ἄγριος⁵⁴⁵, ἄγροικος⁶²²

²⁷ ἀδελφός

brother
• Cf. n. ἀδελφή²⁶⁹

²⁸ αἰχμάλωτος

prisoner of war (αἰχμή 'spear', ἁλίσκεσθαι¹⁰⁸¹
aor. ἁλῶναι)

²⁹ ἄνεμος

wind

³⁰ ἄνθρωπος* [also ἡ]

human being
• Cf. adj. ἀνθρώπινος⁴⁹⁰

³¹ ἄποικος

colonist
• Cf. n. ἀποικία¹⁷⁷, μέτοικος⁷³

³² ἄργυρος

silver
• Cf. n. ἀργύριον³⁸⁷

³³ ἀριθμός

number, amount
• Cf. vb ἀριθμεῖν¹¹⁹⁹

34 ἀστός — citizen, esp. in respect of legal status, opp. ξένος[79] or μέτοικος[73]
- Cf. n. ἄστυ[477], adj. ἀστεῖος[558]

35 αὐτόμολος — deserter
- Cf. vb αὐτομολεῖν[1204]

36 βάρβαρος — non-Greek, hence Persian etc. depending on context; as adj. (-ος -ος -ον), foreign, alien, ἡ βάρβαρος (sc. γῆ) the non-Greek world
- Opp.: Ἕλλην[141]

37 βίος — life, way of life, livelihood, resources
- Cf. vb βιοῦν[1317]

38 βωμός — altar

39 γάμος — marriage, wedding
- Cf. vb γαμεῖν[1207]

40 γεωργός — land-worker, farmer
- Cf. vb γεωργεῖν[1208] (and n. γῆ[280], ἔργον[396])

41 δεσμός — (plur. δεσμοί or neut. δεσμά) bond, bondage, imprisonment
- Cf. n. δεσμωτήριον[393]

42 δῆμος — people, popular government, democratic party or assembly, deme
- Cf. n. δημοκρατία[187], adj. δημόσιος[566]

43 διδάσκαλος — teacher
- Cf. vb διδάσκειν[911]

44 δοῦλος — slave
- Cf. n. δουλεία[189], vb δουλεύειν[915], δουλοῦν[1319] (and n. ἀνδράποδον[386])

45 δρόμος — running (δρόμῳ at a run, at top speed), race (-course)

46 ἔκγονος — offspring, descendant
- Cf. n. πρόγονος[98]

47 ἔλεος — pity, compassion, mercy
- Cf. vb ἐλεεῖν[1219]

48 ἔμπορος — merchant, trader

49 ἐνιαυτός — a year
- Cf. n. ἔτος[428]

50 ἔπαινος — commendation, praise
- Cf. vb ἐπ-αινεῖν[1221]

—ἐπιτήδειος — See adj. ἐπιτήδειος[571]

51 ἑταῖρος — close companion, comrade
- Cf. n. ἑταῖρα[200]

3

52 ἥλιος	*sun*
53 θάνατος	*death, death-sentence*
	• Cf. adj. ἀθάνατος[626]
54 θεός [also ἡ]	*god, fem. goddess*
	• Cf. n. θεά[212], adj. θεῖος[575]
55 θόρυβος	*confused noise, uproar, hubbub, commotion, tumult*
	• Cf. vb θορυβεῖν[1237]
56 θρόνος	*throne, chair* occupied by someone in authority
57 θυμός	*strong feeling* or *emotion,* esp. *spirit, mettle, courage; anger, hot temper*
58 ἰατρός	*doctor*
	• Cf. vb ἰᾶσθαι[1174]
59 ἵππος [also ἡ]	*horse, fem. mare,* ἡ ἵππος also *cavalry*
	• Cf. n. ἱππεῖς[132]
60 καιρός	*opportunity, occasion, (opportune/ critical/ decisive) moment*
	• Cf. n. χρόνος[122]
61 καρπός	*fruit, produce*
62 κατήγορος	*accuser, prosecutor*
	• Cf. vb κατηγορεῖν[1242], n. κατηγορία[216]
63 κίνδυνος	*danger, risk*
	• Cf. vb κινδυνεύειν[967]
64 κλῆρος	*lot, allotment* (of land), *heritable estate*
65 κόλπος	*bay, gulf; lap*
66 κόσμος	*adornment, embellishment; order, arrangement, discipline, system, constitution; universe*
	• Cf. vb κοσμεῖν[1244], adj. κόσμιος[581]
67 κύκλος	*circle*
	• Cf. vb κυκλοῦν[1323]
68 λίθος [also ἡ]	*stone*
69 λιμός	*hunger, starvation, famine*
70 λογισμός	*(numerical) calculation; reasoning, reasoned argument*
	• Cf. vb λογίζεσθαι[1113]
71 λόγος*	*word* etc.
	• Cf. vb λέγειν[981], adj. ἄλογος[630]/ εὔλογος[651], ἀξιόλογος[634]
72 λοιμός	*plague*
73 μέτοικος	*resident alien, metic*
	• Cf. n. ἄποικος[31]

4

74 μισθός — *hire (gen. -οῦ for hire, for a fee), pay, wage*
• Cf. vb μισθοῦν[1324]

75 μῦθος — *saying, tale, story, fiction*

76 νεανίσκος — *young man, young fellow*
• Cf. n. νεανίας[1], adj. νέος[590]

77 νεκρός — *dead body, corpse*

78 νόμος — *custom, convention, observance, regulation, law; the law collectively* οἱ νόμοι or ὁ νόμος
• Cf. adj. νόμιμος[519], vb νομίζειν[998], also n. νομοθέτης[14]

79 ξένος — *guest-friend, guest/ visitor, host; stranger, foreigner, alien; plur. mercenary troops* as opposed to regular citizen-army

80 οἶκος — *house, home, household, esp. estate, inheritance*
• Cf. n. ἄποικος[31], μέτοικος[73]; οἰκία[224]

81 οἶκτος — *pity, compassion*
• Cf. vb οἰκτίρειν[1000]

82 οἶνος — *wine*

83 ὄκνος — *cautious diffidence, hesitation*
• Cf. vb ὀκνεῖν[1257]

84 ὄλεθρος — *destruction; agent of destruction,* applied slightingly to pernicious individuals
• Cf. vb ἀπ-ολλύναι[1333]

85 ὅμιλος — *crowd, throng*
• Cf. n. ὁμιλία[225], vb ὁμιλεῖν[1259]

86 ὄνειρος — *dream* (also -ov, τό; and 3rd declension forms gen. ὀνείρατος, plur. ὀνείρατα etc.)

87 ὅρκος — *oath*
• Cf. vb ἐπι-ορκεῖν[1226]

88 ὅρος — *boundary*

89 οὐρανός — *heaven, sky*

90 ὀφθαλμός — *eye*

91 ὄχλος — *crowd, throng, multitude; annoyance, vexation, trouble* (freq. + παρέχειν[1011], give, cause it)

92 πλοῦτος — *wealth, riches*
• Opp.: πενία[233]
• Cf. adj. πλούσιος[598], vb πλουτεῖν[1265]

93 πόλεμος — *war*
• Opp.: εἰρήνη[289]
• Cf. vb πολεμεῖν[1267], adj./n. πολέμιος[599]

5

94 πόνος	*toil, labour, suffering, hardship, distress* • Cf. vb πονεῖν[1269]
95 πόντος	*sea, open sea*, commonly of particular seas, esp. ὁ Εὔξεινος πόντος, aka ὁ Πόντος
96 πόρος	*pathway, passage; means of providing/* *achieving*, (plur.) *resources, revenue* • Cf. vb πορίζειν[1022], and ctr. n. ἀπορία[179]
97 ποταμός	*river*
98 πρόγονος	*forefather, forebear, ancestor* • Cf. n. ἔκγονος[46]
99 πύργος	*tower*, plur. *city walls, ramparts*
100 σίδηρος	*iron*
101 σῖτος	*grain, bread, food (-supply), provisions* (also τὰ σιτία)
102 σκότος	*darkness* (also τὸ σκότος)
103 στέφανος	*crown, wreath, garland*
104 στρατηγός	*general* • Cf. vb στρατηγεῖν[1274]
105 στρατός	*army, force* • Cf. n. στράτευμα[470]
106 σύμβουλος	*adviser, counsellor, statesman* • Cf. vb συμ-βουλεύειν[1043]
107 σύμμαχος	*ally* • Cf. n. συμμαχία[247]
108 τάφος	*funeral-rites, funeral; grave, tomb*
109 τόπος	*place, region, district* • Cf. adj. ἄτοπος[642]
110 τρόπος	*way* (freq. in adv. phrases, as παντὶ τρόπῳ 'in every way', 'by every/ any means', τοῦτον τὸν τρόπον 'in this manner'), *sort, variety; one's* *character, temperament* (esp. in plur.)
111 τύραννος	*tyrant, autocratic ruler* • Cf. n. τυραννίς[381]
112 υἱός	(gen. υἱοῦ/ υἱέος ~ ὑός gen. ὑοῦ/ ὑέος) *son*
113 ὕπνος	*sleep, period of sleep*
114 φθόνος	*envy, jealousy, resentment* • Cf. vb φθονεῖν[1282], and adj. ἄφθονος[644]
— φίλος	See adj. φίλος[539]
115 φιλόσοφος	*philosopher* • Cf. vb φιλοσοφεῖν[1284]

3

NOUNS

116 φόβος — *fear*
• Cf. vb φοβεῖσθαι[1312], adj. φοβερός[617]

117 φόνος — *murder, homicide*

118 φόρος — *payment,* esp. formal *tribute*

119 φρουρός — *watcher, guard,* plur. *garrison*
• Cf. n. φρουρά[256], vb φρουρεῖν[1287]

120 χαλκός — *bronze*

121 χορός — *chorus, (troop/ company of) dancers, dance*

122 χρόνος — *(period of) time,* χρόνον *for a* (long/ short) *time,* χρόνῳ *in due course, eventually;* v. ὕστερος[614]
• Cf. n. καιρός[160]

123 χρυσός — *gold*

124 ψόγος — *adverse criticism, censure*
• Cf. vb ψέγειν[1077]

125 ψόφος — *noise*
• Cf. vb ψοφεῖν[1290]

126 ὦμος — *shoulder*

2.a/2 Contracted type

127 νοῦς* — *mind*

128 πλοῦς — *journey by sea, voyage*
• Cf. vb πλεῖν[1263]

2.b 'Attic declension'

129 νεώς gen. νεώ — *temple*

3.a -ΕΥΣ, genitive -ΕΩΣ

130 βασιλεύς — *king,* without definite article *King of Persia*

131 ἱερεύς — *priest*
• Cf. adj. ἱερός[577]

132 ἱππεύς (-εῖς) — *horseman,* in plur. *cavalry*
• Cf. n. ἵππος[59]

3.b Other 'third declension' types

133 ἀγών -ῶνος — (athletic/ artistic) *competition, contest; struggle, conflict, pitched battle; legal action, trial*
• Cf. vb ἀγωνίζεσθαι[1078]

134 ἀήρ ἀέρος — *air, atmosphere*

135 ἀνήρ ἀνδρός — *man* (adult male) as opposed to woman or child; *husband*
• Opp.: γυνή[369]

7

	• Cf. adj. ἀνδρεῖος[554], and n. ἀνδρεία[174]; ἄνθρωπος[30]
136 ἄρχων -οντος	archon
	• Cf. vb ἄρχειν[892], n. ἀρχή[274]
137 βοῦς βοός [also ἡ]	ox/ bull, cow; plur. (fem.) cattle
138 γείτων -ονος	neighbour
139 γέλως -ωτος	laughter
	• Cf. vb γελᾶν[1146], adj. γελοῖος[561]
140 γέρων -οντος	old man
141 Ἕλλην -ηνος	Greek
	• Opp.: βάρβαρος[36]
	• Cf. n.ʹΕλλάς[370]
142 ἔρως -ωτος	love ~ sexual desire
	• Cf. n. ἐραστής[5], vb ἐρᾶν[1152]
143 Ζεύς Διός	Zeus (cf. s. μά[1432], νή[1439])
144 ἡγεμών -όνος	leader, guide
	• Cf. vb ἡγεῖσθαι[1304]
145 ἥρως -ωος	hero
146 θήρ θηρός	wild animal, animal
	• Cf. n. θηρίον[399]
147 κῆρυξ κήρυκος	herald
	• Cf. vb κηρύττειν[966]
148 κόλαξ -ακος	flatterer
	• Cf. n. κολακεία[217], vb κολακεύειν[972]
149 κύων κυνός [also ἡ]	dog/ bitch
150 λιμήν -ένος	harbour
151 μάντις -εως	seer
	• Cf. n. μαντεῖον[401], vb μαντεύεσθαι[1115]
152 μάρτυς -υρος	witness
	• Cf. vb μαρτυρεῖν[1250], μαρτύρεσθαι[1116], n. μαρτυρία[220]
153 μήν (or μείς) μηνός	month
154 ὄρνις -ιθος [also ἡ]	bird
155 παῖς παιδός [also ἡ]	child: boy, girl; son, daughter; slave
	• Cf. vb παίζειν[1006]/ παιδεύειν[1005], n. παιδίον[407]; παιδεία[229], παιδιά[230]
156 πατήρ πατρός	father, plur. forefathers
	• Cf. adj. πάτριος[660]/ πατρῷος[596], n. πατρίς[379]
157 ποιμήν -ένος	shepherd
158 πούς ποδός	foot

8

159 πρέσβεις -εων   plur. (of πρέσβυς) *envoys, embassy*
  - Cf. n. πρεσβεία[238], vb πρεσβεύειν[1025]

160 ῥήτωρ -ορος   *speaker, esp. public speaker in ecclesia (often opprobriously), orator, (professional) politician*
  - Cf. n. ῥῆμα[468]

161 σωτήρ -ῆρος   *saviour, deliverer*
  - Cf. n. σωτηρία[250], vb σῴζειν[1046]

162 φυγάς -άδος   *fugitive, exile*
  - Cf. n. φυγή[336], vb φεύγειν[1070]

163 φύλαξ -ακος   *guard, warder, keeper,* plur. often *garrison*
  - Cf. n. φυλακή[337], vb φυλάττειν[1075]

164 χειμών -ῶνος   *winter; bad weather, storm*

B. FEMININE NOUNS

1.a/1 -A (mostly long, sometimes short), genitive -ΑΣ

165 ἀγγελία   *message, report*
  - Cf. vb ἀγγέλλειν[866], n. ἄγγελος[25]

166 ἀγορά   *market place, market, city centre*

167 ἀδικία   *wrongdoing, criminality, injustice*
  - Opp.: δικαιοσύνη[286]
  - Cf. n. ἀδίκημα[455], vb ἀδικεῖν[1182], adj. ἄδικος[624]

168 ἀθυμία   *dejection, depression*
  - Cf. vb ἀθυμεῖν[1184]

169 αἰτία   *responsibility, blame; charge, accusation; cause*
  - Cf. adj. αἴτιος[549] (τὸ -ιον), vb αἰτιᾶσθαι[1168]

170 ἄκρα   *headland, promontory;* κατ᾽ ἄκρας *from top to bottom, completely*
  - Cf. adj. ἄκρος[550]

171 ἀλήθεια   *truth, reality,* τῇ ἀληθείᾳ *truly, really, in point of fact*
  - Cf. adj. ἀληθής[672]

172 ἁμαρτία   *error, fault, sinfulness*
  - Cf. n. ἁμάρτημα[457], vb ἁμαρτάνειν[873]

173 ἀμέλεια   *lack of care, negligence*
  - Cf. vb ἀμελεῖν[1188]

174 ἀνδρεία   *manliness, courage*
  - Opp.: δειλία[186]
  - Cf. adj. ἀνδρεῖος[554]

9

175 ἀπειρία — *inexperience, lack of skill/ expertise* (in: gen.)
- Opp.: ἐμπειρία[194]
- Cf. adj. ἄπειρος[635]

176 ἀπιστία — *distrust, incredulity, (ground for) scepticism, doubt*
- Opp.: πίστις[353]
- Cf. vb ἀπιστεῖν[1195], adj. ἄπιστος[636]

177 ἀποικία — *colony* (settlement 'away from home', ἀπό[750] + οἰκία[224])
- Cf. n. ἄποικος[31]

178 ἀπολογία — *speech in defence*
- Opp.: κατηγορία[216]
- Cf. vb ἀπολογεῖσθαι[1294]

179 ἀπορία — *perplexity, difficulty, embarrassment; + gen., lack, want of*
- Opp.: εὐπορία[204]
- Cf. vb ἀπορεῖν[1197], adj. ἄπορος[637]

180 ἀσέβεια — *impiety*
- Opp.: εὐσέβεια[205]
- Cf. vb ἀσεβεῖν[1201], adj. ἀσεβής[675]

181 ἀσθένεια — *weakness, feeble condition, debilitating disorder, sickness*
- Cf. vb ἀσθενεῖν[1202], adj. ἀσθενής[676]

182 ἀσφάλεια — *safety, security*
- Cf. adj. ἀσφαλής[677]

183 ἀτιμία — *dishonour, esp. deprivation of civic rights, disfranchisement*
- Opp.: τιμή[331]
- Cf. vb ἀτιμοῦν[1315], adj. ἄτιμος[641]

184 βία — *violence, force, coercion,* dat. βίᾳ often *by force, forcibly*
- Cf. vb βιάζεσθαι[1092], adj. βίαιος[559]

185 βοήθεια — *(active) assistance/ support, relief force, reinforcements; legal remedy, redress*
- Cf. vb βοηθεῖν[1206]

186 δειλία — *cowardice*
- Opp.: ἀνδρεία[174]
- Cf. adj. δειλός[494]

187 δημοκρατία — *democracy, democratic constitution*
- Cf. n. δῆμος[42], vb κρατεῖν[1245]

10

188 διάνοια — *intention, plan; way of thinking, mentality, notion, opinion; rational thought, intellectual capacity, intelligence; meaning* of word etc.
- Cf. vb δια-νοεῖσθαι[1298]

189 δουλεία — *slavery, enslavement*
- Cf. vb δουλεύειν[915], δουλοῦν[1319], n. δοῦλος[44]

190 δυστυχία — *bad luck, ill fortune* resulting in *failure*
- Opp.: εὐτυχία[206]
- Cf. vb δυστυχεῖν[1216], adj. δυστυχής[680]

191 δωροδοκία — *taking of bribes*
- Cf. vb δωροδοκεῖν[1217]

192 ἐκκλησία — *assembly*, esp. Athenian *Assembly*

193 ἐλευθερία — *freedom*
- Cf. adj. ἐλεύθερος[569], vb ἐλευθεροῦν[1320]

194 ἐμπειρία — *experience, acquaintance/ expertise* (of/ with/ in: gen.)
- Opp. ἀπειρία[175]
- Cf. adj. ἔμπειρος[647]

195 ἔνδεια — *lack, deficiency, need, neediness, destitution*
- Cf. adj. ἐνδεής[682]

196 ἐξουσία — *power, authority, permission, licence; resources*
- Cf. vb ἐξ-εῖναι[1344], and n. οὐσία[228]

197 ἐπιθυμία — *desire, strong appetite,* often + gen. = for; *sexual desire*
- Cf. vb ἐπιθυμεῖν[1224]

198 ἑσπέρα — *evening; the west*

199 ἑστία — *hearth*

200 ἑταίρα — *female companion; courtesan, prostitute*
- Cf. n. ἑταῖρος[51]

201 εὐδαιμονία — (enviable) *good fortune,* esp. *material prosperity*
- Cf. adj. εὐδαίμων[710]

202 εὐεργεσία — *good deed, service, benefaction*
- Cf. vb εὐεργετεῖν[1230], n. εὐεργέτης[6]

203 εὔνοια — *goodwill, benevolence, loyalty*
- Cf. adj. εὔνους[668]

204 εὐπορία — *ease, easy method of providing* (+ gen.); *abundance, ample supply, affluence*
- Opp.: ἀπορία[179]
- Cf. vb εὐπορεῖν[1231], adj. εὔπορος[652]

11

205 εὐσέβεια	*piety* • Opp.: ἀσέβεια[180] • Cf. vb εὐσεβεῖν[1232], adj. εὐσεβής[686]
206 εὐτυχία	*good fortune, success* • Opp.: δυστυχία[190] • Cf. vb εὐτυχεῖν[1233], adj. εὐτυχής[687]
207 ἔχθρα	*hatred, personal animosity, quarrel, feud* • Cf. adj. ἐχθρός[572]
208 ζημία	*loss, penalty* • Cf. vb ζημιοῦν[1322]
209 ἡλικία	*time of life, age; one's prime, military* or *marriageable age* (also collectively, *men of this age*)
210 ἡμέρα	*day*
211 ἡσυχία	*rest, quiet, inactivity* • Cf. vb ἡσυχάζειν[945], adj. ἡσύχιος[654]/ ἥσυχος[655]
212 θεά	*goddess,* commonly used in expressions involving 'gods [θεοί, see θεός[54]] and goddesses'
213 θύρα	*door* (plur. often (one set of) double doors)
214 θυσία	*sacrifice* • Cf. vb θύειν[949]
215 καρδία	*heart*
216 κατηγορία	*accusation, denunciation* • Opp.: ἀπολογία[178] • Cf. vb κατηγορεῖν[1242], n. κατήγορος[62]
217 κολακεία	*flattery* • Cf. vb κολακεύειν[972], n. κόλαξ[148]
218 λοιδορία	*verbal abuse, invective* • Cf. vb λοιδορεῖν[1247]
219 μανία	*madness* • Cf. vb μαίνεσθαι[1114]
220 μαρτυρία	*testimony, deposition* • Cf. vb μαρτυρεῖν[1250]/ μαρτύρεσθαι[1116], n. μάρτυς[152]
221 μοῖρα	*portion,* esp. *that allotted by higher powers, lot* or *destiny; due measure, that which is natural and right; share of respect due to one, esteem*
222 μωρία	(reprehensible) *folly, stupidity*

NOUNS

223 ναυμαχία	*naval battle* • Cf. vb ναυμαχεῖν[1252]
224 οἰκία	*house, home, household* • Cf. n. ἀποικία[177], οἶκος[80], vb οἰκεῖν[1255]
225 ὁμιλία	*intercourse, association* • Cf. n. ὅμιλος[85], vb ὁμιλεῖν[1259]
226 ὁμολογία	*agreement; point agreed on, admission, concession* • Cf. vb ὁμολογεῖν[1260]
227 ὁμόνοια	*oneness of mind* or *purpose, unanimity, concord*
228 οὐσία	*property, substance; being, essence* • Cf. vb εἶναι[1338], and n. ἐξουσία[196], περιουσία[234], συνουσία[249]
229 παιδεία	*education, culture* • Cf. vb παιδεύειν[1005]
230 παιδιά	*(childish) fun, puerility* • Opp.: σπουδή[322] • Cf. vb παίζειν[1006], n. παῖς[155]
231 παρρησία	*outspokenness, freedom of speech*
232 πεῖρα	*attempt, experiment, enterprise, experience* • Cf. vb πειρᾶσθαι[1178]
233 πενία	*poverty* • Opp.: πλοῦτος[92] • Cf. adj. πένης[717]
234 περιουσία	*surplus, profit, abundance* • Cf. vb περι-εῖναι[1366], and n. οὐσία[228]
235 πλεονεξία	*advantage, gain; undue gain, greedy self-interest* • Cf. vb πλεονεκτεῖν[1264]
236 πολιορκία	*siege* • Cf. vb πολιορκεῖν[1268]
237 πολιτεία	*citizenship; constitution, political system/ regime; government, administration* • Cf. vb πολιτεύεσθαι[1126]
238 πρεσβεία	*embassy* • Cf. n. πρέσβεις[159], vb πρεσβεύειν[1025]
239 προδοσία	*betrayal, treachery* • Cf. vb προ-διδόναι[1367], n. προδότης[19]
240 προθυμία	*enthusiasm, zeal, determination* • Cf. vb προθυμεῖσθαι[1307], adj. πρόθυμος[661]

241 πρόνοια   *foresight, forethought, provident concern;* ἐκ
προνοίας *deliberately, on purpose*
- Cf. vb προ-νοεῖσθαι[1308]

242 ῥᾳθυμία   *taking things (too) easily, indifference,
sluggishness, inertia*
- Cf. adj. ῥᾴθυμος[663]

243 σοφία   (technical) *skill, inventiveness, ingenuity,
brilliance, intelligence, wisdom*
- Cf. adj. σοφός[532], n. σοφιστής[20]

244 στρατεία   *expedition, campaign, military service*
- Cf. n. στρατιά[245], vb στρατεύεσθαι[1131]

245 στρατιά   *army, expeditionary force, campaign*
- Cf. foreg.

246 συγγένεια   *kinship, close relationship;* collectively,
kinsfolk, extended family
- Cf. adj. συγγενής[690]

247 συμμαχία   *alliance*
- Cf. n. σύμμαχος[107]

248 συμφορά   *misfortune, setback, disaster*
- Cf. vb συμ-φέρειν[1044]

249 συνουσία   *a being with, intercourse, association; a
company, party*
- Cf. vb συν-εῖναι[1369], n. οὐσία[228]

250 σωτηρία   *(way/ means/ chance of) safety, salvation,
preservation*
- Cf. n. σωτήρ[161], vb σῴζειν[1046]

251 τιμωρία   *vengeance, retributive punishment, redress;
assistance rendered*
- Cf. vb τιμωρεῖσθαι[1310]

252 ὑποψία   *suspicion*
- Cf. vb ὑποπτεύειν[1066]

253 φιλία   *friendship, friendly relations*
- Cf. vb φιλεῖν[1283], adj. φίλιος[616], φίλος[539]

254 φιλοτιμία   *ambition* or *public-spiritedness,* v. φιλότιμος[665]

255 φλυαρία   *silly talk, nonsense, tomfoolery*
- Cf. vb φλυαρεῖν[1285]

256 φρουρά   *look-out, watch, garrison*
- Cf. vb φρουρεῖν[1287], n. φρουρός[119]

257 χρεία   *need, use, serviceability*
- Cf vb χρῆσθαι[1179]

NOUNS

258 χώρα

place, position (commonly κατὰ χώραν *in position, at one's post*), *station; land, country, territory, area*
- Cf. n. χωρίον⁴¹⁹

259 ὥρα

time of day/ night, *season* of year, *time* of life; *suitable time* (ὥρα + inf., <'it's> *time to* ...')

260 ὠφελία

help, benefit, advantage
- Cf. vb ὠφελεῖν¹²⁹², adj. ὠφέλιμος⁶⁶⁷

1.a/2 Contracted type
261 μνᾶ, gen. μνᾶς

mina (coin)

1.b -A, genitive -ΗΣ
262 ἄμιλλα

contest, race, trial, struggle
- Cf. vb ἀμιλλᾶσθαι¹¹⁷⁰

263 γλῶττα

tongue; language

264 δίαιτα

way of life, life-style, regimen
- Cf. vb διαιτᾶσθαι¹¹⁷¹

265 δόξα

reputation; opinion (παρὰ δόξαν *contrary to expectation* or *to one's belief, convictions;* cf. s. adj. παράδοξος⁶⁵⁹)
- Cf. vb δοξάζειν⁹¹⁴, δοκεῖν¹²¹⁵

266 θάλαττα

sea

267 τόλμα

boldness, daring, excessive boldness, recklessness, brazenness
- Cf. vb τολμᾶν¹¹⁶⁵

268 τράπεζα

table; bank

1.c -Η, genitive -ΗΣ
269 ἀδελφή

sister
- Cf. n. ἀδελφός²⁷

270 αἰσχύνη

shame, dishonour, disgrace, sense of shame
- Cf. vb αἰσχύνεσθαι¹⁰⁸⁰

271 ἀκμή

culminating point, zenith, prime; critical/ most appropriate time

272 ἀνάγκη

necessity, compulsion, coercion, pressure; + acc. and inf., *(it is) necessary that, it follows necessarily that ...*
- Cf. vb ἀναγκάζειν⁸⁷⁶, adj. ἀναγκαῖος⁵⁵³

273 ἀρετή

goodness, excellence, virtue, esp. courage, valour

15

274 ἀρχή*
beginning; rule
• Cf. vb ἄρχειν[892], adj. ἀρχαῖος[557],
n. ἄρχων[136]

275 αὐλή
courtyard
• Cf. vb αὐλίζεσθαι[1090]

276 ἀφορμή
something to set out from, a starting-point; base
of operations, more often basis, resources,
means at one's disposal
• Cf. n. ὁρμή[311], vb ὁρμᾶσθαι[1177]

277 βλάβη
harm, damage
• Cf. adj. βλαβερός[560], vb βλάπτειν[898]

278 βοή
loud cry, shout, yell
• Cf. vb βοᾶν[1145]

279 βουλή
counsel, deliberation; Council
• Cf. vb βουλεύεσθαι[1094]

280 γῆ
earth, land
• Opp.: θάλαττα[266] or οὐρανός[89]

281 γνώμη
intelligence, intellect; judgement, verdict,
opinion; plan, purpose, resolution; attitude
• Cf. vb γιγνώσκειν[900]

282 γραφή
writing, drawing; criminal prosecution,
indictment for a public offence
• Cf. vb γράφειν[901]

283 δαπάνη
cost, expenditure
• Cf. vb δαπανᾶν[1147]

284 διαβολή
slander, misrepresentation; prejudice,
misunderstanding
• Cf. vb δια-βάλλειν[905]

285 διατριβή
occupation, pastime, waste of time/ undue delay
• Cf. vb δια-τρίβειν[908]

286 δικαιοσύνη
honesty, uprightness, righteousness, justice
• Opp.: ἀδικία[167]
• Cf. adj. δίκαιος[567]

287 δίκη*
lawsuit; legal satisfaction
• Cf. vb δικάζειν[912], n. δικαστήριον[394],
δικαστής[3]

288 δραχμή
drachma (coin)

289 εἰρήνη
peace; peace-treaty
• Opp.: πόλεμος[93]

290 εἰσβολή
invasion
• Cf. n. προσβολή[314], vb εἰσ-βάλλειν[920]

291 ἑορτή	*festival, holiday*
292 ἐπιστήμη	*knowledge, systematic/ specialist knowledge* or *expertise, science*
	• Cf. vb ἐπίστασθαι[1382], adj. ἐπιστήμων[709]
293 ἐπιστολή	*verbal* or *written communication, instruction; epistle, letter*
	• Cf. vb ἐπι-στέλλειν[937]
294 εὐνή	*bed*
295 εὐχή	*prayer, vow; wish*
	• Cf. vb εὔχεσθαι[1106]
296 ἥβη	*youth* (time of life)
297 ἡδονή	*pleasure, enjoyment*
	• Cf. vb ἥδεσθαι[1107], adj. ἡδύς[700]
298 κεφαλή	*head*
299 κλοπή	*theft*
	• Cf. vb κλέπτειν[970], n. κλέπτης[10]
300 κόρη	*girl*
301 κρήνη	*spring, fountain*
302 κώμη	*village*
303 λύπη	*pain, grief, distress, annoyance*
	• Cf. vb λυπεῖν[1248]
304 μάχη	*battle*
	• Cf. vb μάχεσθαι[1117], n. ναυμαχία[223]
305 μελέτη	*practice, exercise, training*
	• Cf. vb μελετᾶν[1155]
306 μεταβολή	*change, transition*
	• Cf. vb μετα-βάλλειν[991]
307 μηχανή	*device, (siege-) engine, plur. ploys, means, ways and means*
	• Cf. vb μηχανᾶσθαι[1176]
308 μνήμη	*remembrance,* (faculty of) *memory*
	• Cf. vb μιμνήσκεσθαι[1120]
309 νίκη	*victory*
	• Cf. vb νικᾶν[1156]
310 ὀργή	*temperament, mood, esp. angry mood, anger*
	• Cf. vb ὀργίζεσθαι[1123]
311 ὁρμή	*overwhelming desire, sudden impulse*
	• Cf. n. ἀφορμή[276], vb ὁρμᾶσθαι[1177]
312 παρασκευή	*act of preparing/ means of providing, state of preparedness, product of preparation (properly*

	equipped force, equipment, resources etc.)
	• Cf. vb παρα-σκευάζειν[1010]
313 πληγή	*stroke, blow,* plur. often *a beating*
	• Cf. vb ἐκ-πλήττειν[924]
314 προσβολή	*assault, attack*
	• Cf. n.εἰσβολή[290], vb προσ-βάλλειν[1026]
315 πύλη	*gate,* plur. often *city-gates*
316 ῥώμη	*physical strength, energy; mental energy, confidence*
317 σελήνη	*moon*
318 σιγή	*silence,* σιγῇ *in silence*
	• Cf. vb σιγᾶν[1161]
319 σιωπή	*silence,* σιωπῇ *in silence*
	• Cf. vb σιωπᾶν[1162]
320 σκήνη	*tent; stage-building, stage*
321 σπονδή (σπονδαί)	plur. *treaty, truce*
	• Cf. vb σπένδεσθαι[1130]
322 σπουδή*	*hot haste* etc.
	• Opp.: παιδιά[230]
	• Cf. vb σπουδάζειν[1035], adj. σπουδαῖος[607]
323 στήλη	*stele, stone slab, column*
324 συγγνώμη	*forbearance, pardon, forgiveness;* συγγνώμην ἔχειν *pardon* one (dat.; for: gen.)
	• Cf. vb συγγιγνώσκειν[1038]
325 συνθήκη (συνθῆκαι)	plur. *formal agreement, covenant, treaty*
	• Cf. vb συν-τίθεσθαι[1387]
326 σχολή	*leisure, spare time,* dat. σχολῇ *at a leisurely pace* or *hardly*
	• Cf. vb σχολάζειν[1045]
327 σωφροσύνη	*prudence, self-control* etc. cf. s. adj. σώφρων[711], vb σωφρονεῖν[1277]
328 ταραχή	*disorder, upheaval, disruption, turmoil*
	• Cf. vb ταράττειν[1047]
329 τελευτή	*end;* w. or without βίου, *end of one's life, death*
	• Cf. adj. τελευταῖος[610], vb τελευτᾶν[1163]
330 τέχνη	*art, skill, craft, trade, profession*
331 τιμή	*honour, respect; worth, value*
	• Opp.: ἀτιμία[183]
	• Cf. vb τιμᾶν[1164], adj. τίμιος[611]
332 τροπή	*putting to flight, routing, rout*
	• Cf. vb τρέπειν[1054]

18

333 τροφή — *nourishment, food, provisions; nurturing, nurture*
- Cf. vb τρέφειν[1055]

334 τύχη — *chance, fortune (good or bad)*
- Cf. vb τυγχάνειν[1057]

335 ὕλη — *woodland, undergrowth, a wood; felled timber, firewood*

336 φυγή — *flight, escape; exile*
- Cf. vb φεύγειν[1070], n. φυγάς[162]

337 φυλακή — *guarding; guard, garrison*
- Cf. n. φύλαξ[163], vb φυλάττειν[1075]

338 φυλή — *tribe*

339 φωνή — *voice, speech, language*

340 ψυχή — *life, soul, inner self, mind/ feelings*, often opp. body, as εὖ παρεσκευασμένοι καὶ τὰς ψυχὰς καὶ τὰ σώματα, 'well prepared both mentally and physically'

341 ᾠδή — *song*
- Cf. vb ᾄδειν[869]

2.a -ΟΣ, genitive -ΟΥ

342 ἤπειρος — *land, mainland, continent*

343 νῆσος — *island*

344 νόσος — *illness, disease*
- Cf. vb νοσεῖν[1253]

345 ὁδός — *way, road, journey*

346 ψῆφος — *pebble, counter; vote*
- Cf. n. ψήφισμα[476], vb ψηφίζεσθαι[1140]

2.b 'Attic declension'

347 ἕως gen. ἕω — *dawn; the east*

3.a -ΙΣ, genitive -ΕΩΣ

348 ἀκρόπολις — *acropolis*
- Cf. adj. ἄκρος[550], n. πόλις[355]

349 ἀπόκρισις — *answer, response*
- Cf. vb ἀπο-κρίνεσθαι[1088]

350 δύναμις — *power* (also actual *force, armed forces*), *capacity* (κατὰ δύναμιν *to the best of one's ability, as far as one can*, cf. s. δυνατός[497]);

	influence; meaning
	• Cf. vb δύνασθαι¹³⁸¹
351 ἔκπληξις	*consternation, panic, bewilderment, severe* *shock*
	• Cf. vb ἐκ-πλήττειν⁹²⁴
352 ὄψις	*appearance, countenance, sight, power of sight,* *vision*
353 πίστις	*pledge, assurance, guarantee*
	• Cf. vb πιστεύειν¹⁰²¹, adj. πιστός⁵²⁷
354 ποίησις	*act of producing, production; writing of poetry,* actual *poetic composition*
	• Cf. n. ποίημα⁴⁶⁶, ποιητής¹⁷, vb ποιεῖν¹²⁶⁶
355 πόλις	*city, state, country*
	• Cf. n. πολιτεία²³⁷, πολίτης¹⁸, and adj. πολιτικός⁵²⁸; n. ἀκρόπολις³⁴⁸
356 πρᾶξις	*transacting, carrying out, execution, activity,* *action*
	• Cf. vb πράττειν¹⁰²³, n. πρᾶγμα⁴⁶⁷
357 προαίρεσις	*preferred course of action, deliberate policy,* ἐκ προαιρέσεως *deliberately*
	• Cf. vb προ-αιρεῖσθαι¹³⁰⁶
358 πρόφασις	*(alleged) reason, pretext, cause; (true) reason,* *motive, cause*
359 στάσις	*faction, factional strife*
	• Cf. vb στασιάζειν¹⁰³⁶
360 σύνεσις	*sagacity, intelligence*
	• Cf. adj. συνετός⁵³⁴
361 τάξις	*post, place in battle-line,* often found in expression λείπειν⁹⁸² τὴν τάξιν
362 ὕβρις*	*outrageous behaviour*
	• Cf. vb ὑβρίζειν¹⁰⁵⁹
363 ὑπόσχεσις	*promise, undertaking*
	• Cf. vb ὑπ-ισχνεῖσθαι¹³¹¹
364 φρόνησις	*intelligence, prudence, wisdom*
	• Cf. adj. φρόνιμος⁶⁶⁶
365 φύσις	*nature, natural disposition,* κατὰ φύσιν (or φύσει) *naturally,* opp. παρὰ φύσιν
	• Cf. vb φύειν¹⁰⁷⁴

3.b Other 'third declension' types

366 αἰδώς -οῦς	awe, respect, self-respect, sense of shame, embarrassment
	• Cf. adj. ἀναιδής[674]
367 ἀσπίς -ίδος	shield
368 γραῦς γραός	old woman
369 γυνή γυναικός	woman, wife
	• Opp.: ἀνήρ[135]
370 Ἑλλάς -άδος	Greece
	• Cf. n. Ἕλλην[141]
371 ἐλπίς -ίδος	expectation, hope
	• Cf. vb ἐλπίζειν[928]
372 ἔρις -ιδος	strife, quarrel, wrangling, rivalry, discord
373 ἐσθής -ῆτος	clothing, clothes, dress
374 θυγάτηρ θυγατρός	daughter
375 ἰσχύς -ύος	strength, power, validity
	• Cf. vb ἰσχύειν[951], adj. ἰσχυρός[578]
376 μήτηρ μητρός	mother
377 ναῦς νεώς	ship (cf. under μακρός[585])
	• Cf. vb ναυμαχεῖν[1252], and n. ναυμαχία[223], ναύτης[13], ναυτικόν[403]
378 νύξ νυκτός	night
	• Cf. adv. νύκτωρ[810]
379 πατρίς -ίδος	fatherland
	• Cf. n. πατήρ[156]
380 τριήρης -ους	trireme, warship
381 τυραννίς -ίδος	tyranny, autocratic rule
	• Cf. n. τύραννος[111]
382 φλόξ φλογός	flame
383 χάρις* -ιτος	favour, gratitude
	• Cf. vb χαρίζεσθαι[1138]
384 χείρ χειρός	hand, arm
	• Cf. vb ἐπι-χειρεῖν[1228], χειροτονεῖν[1288]

C. NEUTER NOUNS

2 -ON, genitive -ΟΥ

385 ἆθλον	prize awarded in a contest/ competition (sts metaphorical)
386 ἀνδράποδον	slave, of a captive enslaved in war (irrespective

21

of previous status); or generally, = δοῦλος[44]

• Cf. vb ἀνδραποδίζειν[878]

387 ἀργύριον   *(sum of) money, cash*

• Cf. n. ἄργυρος[32]

388 βιβλίον/ βυβλίον   *book*

389 γυμνάσιον   *gymnasium*

• Cf. vb γυμνάζεσθαι[1096], adj. γυμνός[493]

390 δάκρυον   *tear* shed in grief etc.

• Cf. vb δακρύειν[902]

391 δεῖπνον   *meal, dinner, supper*

• Cf. vb δειπνεῖν[1211]

392 δένδρον   *tree*

393 δεσμωτήριον   *prison*

• Cf. n. δεσμός[41]

394 δικαστήριον   *lawcourt*

• Cf. vb δικάζειν[912], n. δικαστής[3]

395 δῶρον   *gift, present; bribe*

• Cf. n. δωροδοκία[191], vb δωροδοκεῖν[1217]

396 ἔργον*   *work* etc.

• Cf. vb ἐργάζεσθαι[1105], and adj. ἀργός[640], n. εὐεργέτης[6]

397 ζῷον   *animal, creature; artistic image, figure*

• Cf. vb ζῆν[1167]

398 θέατρον   *theatre*

• Cf. n. θεατής[7], vb θεᾶσθαι[1173]

399 θηρίον   *wild animal, animal*

• Cf. n. θήρ[146]

400 ἱμάτιον   *outer garment, cloak* or *coat;* plur. *clothes*

401 μαντεῖον   *oracle* (site of delivery or actual response)

• Cf. vb μαντεύεσθαι[1115], n. μάντις[151]

402 μέτρον   (dry or liquid) *measure, measured amount, distance; due measure, reasonable or acceptable limit, the mean*

• Cf. adj. μέτριος[586]

403 ναυτικόν   *navy, fleet*

• Cf. n. ναῦς[377], ναύτης[13]

404 νῶτον   one's *back; the rear* (κατὰ νώτου *in the rear*)

405 ξύλον   (piece of) *wood, timber* (often plur.)

— ὄνειρον   See ὄνειρος[86]

406 ὅπλον (-α)   plur. *(heavy) arms, weapons*

• Cf. n. ὁπλῖται[16], vb ὁπλίζειν[1003]

407 παιδίον	(small/ young) *child* • Cf. n. παῖς[155]
408 πεδίον	*tract of level ground, plain*
409 πλοῖον	*boat, vessel, craft* • Cf. n. πλοῦς[128], vb πλεῖν[1263]
410 πρόσωπον	*face, countenance*
411 σημεῖον	*sign, signal; indication, proof* • Cf. vb σημαίνειν[1033]
— σιτίον/ plur. -ία	See σῖτος[101]
412 στάδιον	(plur. στάδια or masc. στάδιοι) *stade*
413 στρατόπεδον	*encampment; army, force, troops* • Cf. vb στρατοπεδεύεσθαι[1132]
414 τάλαντον	*talent* (unit of weight or money)
415 τεκμήριον	*item of evidence* (plur. *body of evidence*), *proof,* *indication, sign* • Cf. vb τεκμαίρεσθαι[1135]
416 τόξον	*bow* (weapon) • Cf. n. τοξότης[23]
417 τροπαῖον	*trophy* to commemorate enemy defeat • Cf. n. τροπή[332]
418 φάρμακον	*drug, medicine, remedy; poison*
419 χωρίον	*place, spot, position*, plur. often *ground,* *terrain; estate, farm* • Cf. n. χώρα[258]

3.a -ΟΣ, genitive -ΟΥΣ

420 ἄνθος	*blossom, flower*
421 βέλος	*missile* • Cf. vb βάλλειν[897]
422 γένος	*race, family, class, kind, category, sex* (as τὸ τῶν ἀνδρῶν γ. 'the male sex')
423 δέος	*fear, alarm* • Cf. adj. ἀδεής[669], vb δεδιέναι/δεδοικέναι[1373]
424 ἔθνος	*nation, people; social class*
425 ἔθος	*custom, habit*
426 εἶδος	*form,* [Platonic] *ideal form, figure; class, kind,* *species, variety*
427 ἔπος	*utterance, word*, common in expression ὡς ἔπος εἰπεῖν *practically, just about*
428 ἔτος	*year* • Cf. n. ἐνιαυτός[49]

429 εὖρος	*width, breadth*
	• Cf. adj. εὑρύς[699]
430 ἦθος	*custom; disposition, character, characteristic*
431 θάρρος/ θάρσος	*courage, confidence*
	• Cf. vb θαρρεῖν/ θαρσεῖν[1235]
432 θέρος	*summer* (often of campaigning season)
433 θράσος	*over-boldness, audacity, insolence*
	• Cf. adj. θρασύς[703]
434 κάλλος	*beauty*
	• Cf. adj. καλός[507]
435 κέρδος	*gain, profit, advantage*
	• Cf. vb κερδαίνειν[965]
436 κράτος	*strength, power* (κατὰ κράτος *by applying* <*all one's*> *strength*, of all-out fighting or storming)
	• Cf. vb κρατεῖν[1245], and adj. καρτερός[580]
437 μέγεθος	*magnitude, extent, size, stature, severity, intensity* etc.
	• Cf. adj. μέγας[715]
438 μέλος	*limb; song, lyric poem*
439 μέρος	*part* (acc. of respect μέρος τι 'in part', τὸ σὸν μέρος 'for your part', 'as far as you are concerned'), *portion, one's turn* (ἐν μέρει 'in turn, by turns')
440 μῆκος	*length*
	• Cf. adj. μακρός[585]
441 ξίφος	*sword*
442 ὄνειδος	*reproach*
	• Cf. vb ὀνειδίζειν[1001]
443 ὄρος	*mountain*
444 ὄφελος	*use, benefit, good*
445 πάθος	*experience,* esp. *bad experience, setback, disaster; condition, property; emotion*
	• Cf. vb πάσχειν[1013] (aor. inf. παθεῖν)
446 πέλαγος	*open sea*
447 πλῆθος	*great number, crowd ~ the greater number, superior numbers, majority, the people/ populace; magnitude, extent, amount, quantity*
448 σκεῦος	*vessel, implement;* commonly in plur., *utensils, implements, equipment, gear, baggage*
— σκότος	See σκότος[102]

24

449 τάχος	*speed, rapidity* • Cf. adj. ταχύς[706]
450 τεῖχος	*wall, fort, fortification* • Cf. n. τείχισμα[473], vb τειχίζειν[1050]
451 τέλος*	*completion, fulfilment, execution* etc. • Cf. vb τελεῖν[1279]
452 ὕψος	*height* • Cf. adj. ὑψηλός[537]
453 ψεῦδος	*lie, falsehood* • Cf. vb ψεύδεσθαι[1139], adj. ψευδής[694]

3.b -A, genitive -ΑΤΟΣ

454 ἄγαλμα	*statue, esp. in honour of a god*
455 ἀδίκημα	*act of injustice, crime* • Cf. n. ἀδικία[167], vb ἀδικεῖν[1182], adj. ἄδικος[624]
456 αἷμα	*blood, bloodshed*
457 ἁμάρτημα	*error, sinful act, offence* • Cf. n. ἁμαρτία[172], vb ἁμαρτάνειν[873]
458 γράμμα	*letter of alphabet;* plur. *set of letters, written characters* or *writings,* hence *inscription, documents, records* etc. • Cf. vb γράφειν[901], n. γραφή[282]
459 δρᾶμα	*drama, play* • Cf. vb δρᾶν[1148]
460 ἐπιτήδευμα	*pursuit, activity, (habitual) practice;* plur. *habits, way of life* • Cf. vb ἐπιτηδεύειν[938], adj. ἐπιτήδειος[571]
461 κτῆμα	*possession,* plur. *property* • Cf. vb κτᾶσθαι[1175]
462 οἰκοδόμημα	*building, structure* • Cf. vb οἰκοδομεῖν[1256]
463 ὄνομα	*name, word, term* • Cf. vb ὀνομάζειν[1002]
464 παράδειγμα	*example, lesson, illustration, proof*
465 πνεῦμα	*blast, breeze, breath*
466 ποίημα	*product; poem* • Cf. n. ποίησις[354], ποιητής[17], vb ποιεῖν[1266]
467 πρᾶγμα	*thing, affair, business, pursuit, negotiation* etc.; *trouble,* παῦσαι σαυτῷ παρέχων πράγματα,

25

	'stop making trouble for yourself'
	• Cf. vb πράττειν[1023], n. πρᾶξις[356]
468 ῥῆμα	something said: saying, expression, phrase, word
	• Cf. n. ῥήτωρ[160]
469 στόμα	mouth
470 στράτευμα	army, fighting force
	• Cf. vb στρατεύεσθαι[1131], n. στρατός[105]
471 σχῆμα	shape, figure, (characteristic) form; outward form, bearing, posture
472 σῶμα	body, one's person
473 τείχισμα	fortification, fort
	• Cf. vb τειχίζειν[1050], n. τεῖχος[450]
474 τραῦμα	wound
475 χρῆμα (χρήματα)	plur. goods, money
	• Cf. vb χρῆσθαι[1179]
476 ψήφισμα	decree
	• Cf. vb ψηφίζεσθαι[1140], n. ψῆφος[346]

3.c Other 'third declension' types

477 ἄστυ -εως	city, town (built-up area, opp. countryside)
	• Cf. n. ἀστός[34], adj. ἀστεῖος[558]
478 γέρας -ως	prerogative, privilege
479 γῆρας γήρως	old age
480 γόνυ -ατος	knee
481 δόρυ -ατος	spear
482 ἔαρ ἦρος	spring (season)
483 κέρας -ατος/ -ως	horn; wing of army/ fleet
484 κρέας κρέως	(portion/ ration of) meat
485 οὖς ὠτός	ear
486 πῦρ πυρός	fire
487 ὕδωρ ὕδατος	water, rain, rainfall
488 φῶς φωτός	light

II. ADJECTIVES

[Many *pronouns* are used adjectivally: these are listed under V below]

A.1.a -ΟΣ: fem. -Η, neut. -ΟΝ (fem. occasionally -ΟΣ in those labelled §)

489 ἀγαθός*
    good etc.
- Comp. ἀμείνων, βελτίων, κρείττων
- Sup. ἄριστος, βέλτιστος, κράτιστος
- Adv. εὖ[791]
- Opp.: κακός[506]

490 ἀνθρώπινος§
    human, τἀνθρώπινα *human affairs, the world of man*
- Opp.: θεῖος[575]
- Cf. n. ἄνθρωπος[30]

491 ἄσμενος
    with satisfaction, glad(ly), e.g. ἄσμενοι τοῦτο ποιοῦσιν (cf. on adj. ἄκων[712])

492 αὐτόματος
    self-acting, happening without external agency/ visible cause, natural, spontaneous
    τὸ αὐτόματον *accident*
    ἀπὸ ταὐτομάτου *accidentally, by coincidence*

493 γυμνός
    (stark) naked, unclad or *partly-clad, exposed;* + gen., *stripped, divested* of something
- Cf. vb γυμνάζεσθαι[1096], n. γυμνάσιον[389]

494 δειλός
    cowardly, craven
- Opp.: ἀνδρεῖος[554]
- Cf. n. δειλία[186]

495 δεινός*
    terrible, formidable etc.

496 δῆλος*
    clear, obvious
- Opp.: ἄδηλος[623]
- Cf. vb δηλοῦν[1318]

497 δυνατός
    able, capable, powerful, influential; possible (κατὰ τὸ δυνατόν *so far as possible,* cf. s. n. δύναμις[350]), *practicable,* often with inf.
- Opp.: ἀδύνατος[625]
- Cf. vb δύνασθαι[1381]

498 ἐμός
    my (plur.ἡμέτερος[573]), commonly with some degree of emphasis

499 ἔσχατος	*furthest, remotest, latest, last;* of misfortunes etc., *ultimate, extreme, worst imaginable*
500 θαυμαστός	*marvellous, amazing, wonderful, extraordinary* • Cf. adj. θαυμάσιος[574], vb θαυμάζειν[947]
501 θερμός	*hot* • Opp.: ψυχρός[618]
502 θνητός	*mortal* • Opp.: ἀθάνατος[626]
503 ἱκανός	*adequate, sufficient;* + inf., *competent to do, capable of, up to* doing
504 ἴσος	*equal* (to: dat.), *equally* or *equitably divided* • Cf. adv. ἴσως[795]
505 καινός	*new, novel, unheard of, strange* • Opp.: ἀρχαῖος[557]
506 κακός*	*bad* etc. • Comp. etc: see Supp.
507 καλός*	*admirable, honourable* etc. • Comp. καλλίων, Sup. κάλλιστος • Opp.: αἰσχρός[548] • Cf. n. κάλλος[434]
508 κενός	*empty, unoccupied, unmanned; empty-handed; empty, idle, ineffectual* • Opp.: μεστός[517], πλήρης[688]
509 κοῖλος	*hollow*
510 κοινός	*common, shared, public, belonging to the community;* τὰ κοινά *public authorities, government, public funds, public affairs/ life;* adv. κοινῇ *in common, jointly*
511 κοῦφος	*light, slight, lightweight, empty, vain*
512 λεπτός	*fine, thin, delicate;* (intellectually) *refined, subtle* • Opp.: παχύς[705]
513 λευκός	*white* • Opp.: μέλας[716]
514 λοιπός	*left over, remaining; future,* τὸ λοιπόν *in future, henceforth* • Cf. vb λείπειν[982]
515 μαλακός	*soft* to the touch; of persons, *soft, faint-hearted, cowardly*

28

516 μέσος   *in/ at the middle, mid; middle of:* μέσος + article + n., διὰ μέσης τῆς νήσου, 'across the middle of the island'

517 μεστός   *full, filled* (of/ with: gen.)
- Opp.: κενός[508]

518 μόνος   *only, alone;* οὐ μόνον ... ἀλλὰ καί *not only ... but also,* μόνον οὐ *all but* cf. ὅσον[1455] οὐ

519 νόμιμος§   *in accordance with/ observant of custom* or *law, legitimate;* τὰ νόμιμα *observances, standards of conduct sanctioned by usage*
- Cf. n. νόμος[78], vb νομίζειν[998]

520 ὀλίγος*   *little, small* etc.
- Comp. ἐλάττων (cf. s. μικρός[587]), Sup. ὀλίγιστος
- Opp.: πολύς[718]
- Cf. adv. ὀλιγάκις[816], vb ὀλιγωρεῖν[1258]

521 ὅλος*   *whole*

522 ὀρθός   *upright, straight, right, correct, proper*

523 παντοδαπός   *of every kind, description*
- Cf. adj. παντοῖος[595]

524 πεζός   *on foot/ land, land-:* πεζός w. or without στρατός = land-force, infantry = πεζοί

525 περιττός   *out of the ordinary, extraordinary; superfluous, excessive*

526 πιθανός   *persuasive, plausible*
- Cf. vb πείθειν[1016]

527 πιστός   *to be relied on, trustworthy, credible;* τὸ πιστόν *pledge*
- Opp.: ἄπιστος[636]
- Cf. vb πιστεύειν[1021], n. πίστις[353]

528 πολιτικός   *relating to/ consisting of citizens, citizen-; relating to state/ state-administration, civic, political, public,* τὰ πολιτικά *affairs of state*
- Cf. n. πολιτεία[237], πολίτης[18], πόλις[355]

529 πρῶτος   *first, foremost, leading;* adv. πρῶτον *in the first place,* also τὸ πρῶτον or τὰ πρῶτα, *first of all, at first, initially*
- Cf. adj. πρότερος[602]

530 σεμνός   *august, reverend; haughty, pompous, pretentious*

[531] σός	*your* (sing. reference, plur. ὑμέτερος[612]), used with varying degrees of emphasis
[532] σοφός	*skilful, accomplished, brilliant, ingenious, wise* • Opp.: ἀμαθής[673] • Cf. n. σοφία[243], σοφιστής[20]
[533] στενός	*narrow* • Opp.: εὐρύς[699]
[534] συνετός	*sagacious, intelligent* • Cf. n. σύνεσις[360]
[535] συχνός	*long, much, a great deal of,* plur. *many, numerous*
[536] ταπεινός	*low, humble*
[537] ὑψηλός	*high, elevated* • Cf. n. ὕψος[452]
[538] φαῦλος§	*trivial, petty, ordinary, undistinguished, of indifferent quality, mediocre, poor, bad*
[539] φίλος	*dear, welcome, pleasing,* often w. dat.; also φίλος, ὁ *friend* • Opp.: ἐχθρός[572] • Cf. vb φιλεῖν[1283], n. φιλία[253], adj. φίλιος[616]
[540] χαλεπός	*difficult, hard to deal with, trying, dangerous, severe* etc. • Opp.: ῥᾴδιος[603]
[541] χρήσιμος§	*useful* • Cf. vb χρῆσθαι[1179]
[542] χρηστός	*good* • Opp.: πονηρός[600]
[543] ψιλός	*bare,* often *light-armed*
[544] ὠμός	*raw, uncooked; cruel, brutal, vicious, inhumane*

A.1.b -ΟΣ: fem. -A, neut. -ON (entries marked §: occasionally -ΟΣ in fem.)

[545] ἄγριος§	*wild, untamed, uncultivated; savage, fierce, uncivilised* • Opp.: ἥμερος[653] • Cf. n. ἀγρός[26], adj. ἄγροικος[622]
[546] ἄθλιος	*miserable, wretched, abject; good-for-nothing, unprincipled* (cf. s. adj. μοχθηρός[588])
[547] ἀθρόος§	*massed* or *concentrated, all together, in a body* • Cf. vb ἀθροίζειν[870]
[548] αἰσχρός	(physically) *ugly,* (morally) *shameful,*

ADJECTIVES

disgraceful, disreputable, scandalous
• Comp. αἰσχίων, Sup. αἴσχιστος
• Opp.: καλός⁵⁰⁷

549 αἴτιος*
responsible, to blame
• Opp.: ἀναίτιος⁶³¹
• Cf. n. αἰτία¹⁶⁹, vb αἰτιᾶσθαι¹¹⁶⁸

550 ἄκρος*
(relating to) the top, surface of etc.
• Cf. n. ἄκρα¹⁷⁰, ἀκρόπολις³⁴⁸

551 ἀλλοῖος
of another or different kind
• Cf. ἄλλος¹³⁹¹

552 ἀλλότριος
belonging to someone else, alien, foreign, extraneous
• Opp.: οἰκεῖος⁵⁹¹
• Cf. ἄλλος¹³⁹¹

553 ἀναγκαῖος
applying force, coercive; necessary, indispensable, essential; related (by blood)
• Cf. vb ἀναγκάζειν⁸⁷⁶, n. ἀνάγκη²⁷²

554 ἀνδρεῖος
behaving like a man, brave, courageous
• Opp.: δειλός⁴⁹⁴
• Cf. n. ἀνδρεία¹⁷⁴, ἀνήρ¹³⁵

555 ἄξιος*
worthy, deserving
• Opp.: ἀνάξιος⁶³²
• Cf. vb ἀξιοῦν¹³¹⁴, adj. ἀξιόλογος⁶³⁴

556 ἀριστερός
left, on the left; ἀριστερά w. or without χείρ left hand
• Opp.: δεξιός⁵⁶⁴
• Cf. adj. σκαιός⁶⁰⁴

557 ἀρχαῖος
ancient, old, old-fashioned, antiquated; former; τὸ ἀρχαῖον in ancient/ early times
• Opp.: καινός⁵⁰⁵
• Cf. n. ἀρχή²⁷⁴; adj. παλαιός⁵⁹⁴

558 ἀστεῖος
relating to the ἄστυ: clever, witty, charming, agreeable
• Opp.: ἄγροικος⁶²²
• Cf. n. ἀστός³⁴, ἄστυ⁴⁷⁷

559 βίαιος§
involving or employing force/ violence, violent
• Cf. n. βία¹⁸⁴, vb βιάζεσθαι¹⁰⁹²

560 βλαβερός
injurious, harmful
• Cf. n. βλάβη²⁷⁷, vb βλάπτειν⁸⁹⁸

561 γελοῖος
provoking laughter, laughable, ludicrous
• Cf. vb γελᾶν¹¹⁴⁶, n. γέλως¹³⁹

31

562 γενναῖος	noble (-born/ -minded)
563 γνήσιος	true-born, legitimate, genuine, authentic
564 δεξιός	on the right (ἡ δεξιά right hand); dexterous, skilful
	• Opp.: ἀριστερός[556]
565 δεύτερος	second, next
566 δημόσιος	belonging to the people or state, public; τὸ δημόσιον commonly = treasury, δημοσίᾳ publicly, at public expense
	• Opp.: ἴδιος[576]
	• Cf. n. δῆμος[42]
567 δίκαιος*	honest, upright, just
	• Opp.: ἄδικος[624]
	• Cf. n. δικαιοσύνη[286], δίκη[287]
568 ἑκούσιος§	voluntary, intentional
	• Opp.: ἀκούσιος[628]
	• Cf. adj. ἑκών[714]
569 ἐλεύθερος	free
	• Cf. n. ἐλευθερία[193], vb ἐλευθεροῦν[1320]
570 ἐναντίος*	opposite, opposing
	• Cf. vb ἐναντιοῦσθαι[1326]
571 ἐπιτήδειος*	useful, serviceable etc.
	• Cf. vb ἐπιτηδεύειν[938], n. ἐπιτήδευμα[460]
572 ἐχθρός	hostile; as noun, (personal) enemy
	• Opp.: φίλος[539]
	• Cf. n. ἔχθρα[207]
573 ἡμέτερος	our (sing. ἐμός[498])
574 θαυμάσιος	marvellous, amazing, wonderful, extraordinary
	• Cf. adj. θαυμαστός[500], vb θαυμάζειν[947]
575 θεῖος	divine, godlike
	• Opp.: ἀνθρώπινος[490]
	• Cf. n. θεός[54]
576 ἴδιος§	private, personal, individual; ἰδίᾳ privately, on a personal level
	• Opp.: δημόσιος[566]
	• Cf. n. ἰδιώτης[8]
577 ἱερός	sacred; τὸ ἱερόν temple, sanctuary, τὰ ἱερά sacrifices, rites
	• Cf. n. ἱερεύς[131]
578 ἰσχυρός	strong, powerful, violent, severe; effective, valid
	• Opp.: ἀσθενής[676]

ADJECTIVES

	• Cf. vb ἰσχύειν[951], n. ἰσχύς[375], vb ἰσχυρίζεσθαι[1108]
579 καθαρός	clean, pure, clear, unobstructed; with clean hands, free from guilt or pollution • Cf. vb καθαίρειν[952]
580 καρτερός	strong, powerful, potent, overpowering, intense • Cf. vb καρτερεῖν[1240], n. κράτος[436]
581 κόσμιος	moderate, decently behaved, law-abiding • Cf. vb κοσμεῖν[1244], n. κόσμος[66]
582 κύριος	in or exercising control, having authority (of/over: gen.); valid — As noun, master, head of household (often in capacity of legal guardian) • Opp.: ἄκυρος[629]
583 λαμπρός	brilliant, illustrious, celebrated, distinguished; conspicuous, manifest, patent
584 μακάριος§	Much like εὐδαίμων[710], q.v.
585 μακρός	long (ναῦς μακρά warship), remote, loud and long; μακρῷ w. Comp. or Sup. by far • Opp.: βραχύς[698] • Cf. n. μῆκος[440]
586 μέτριος§	moderate, reasonable, decently behaved • Cf. n. μέτρον[402]
587 μικρός*	(also σμικρός) small etc. • Comp. ἐλάττων (smaller, fewer, less) • Sup. ἐλάχιστος (smallest, shortest, fewest) • Opp.: μέγας[715]
588 μοχθηρός	in a sorry state, of persons (miserable, wretched; alternatively good for nothing, reprobate, villainous, cf. s. adj. ἄθλιος[546]) or things (in bad condition)
589 μυρίος	countless, infinite; μύριοι -αι -α [so accented] as numeral, 10,000
590 νέος*	young, youthful • Cf. adv. νεωστί[809], n. νεανίας[1]/ νεανίσκος[76]
591 οἰκεῖος	one's own, personal, private; (closely) related, akin, οἱ οἰκεῖοι relatives • Opp.: ἀλλότριος[552] • Cf. n. οἶκος[80]
592 ὅμοιος	like, resembling, + dat.
593 ὅσιος§	sanctioned by the gods or by divine law; pious, righteous • Opp.: ἀνόσιος[633]

594 παλαιός — old, of long standing, going back in time (not necessarily a long way back)
• Cf. adv. πάλαι[828], and adj. ἀρχαῖος[557]

595 παντοῖος — of every kind/ description
• Cf. adj. παντοδαπός[523]

596 πατρῷος — belonging to/ inherited from one's father (τὰ πατρῷα father's estate, patrimony), hereditary
• Cf. adj. πάτριος[660]

597 πικρός — bitter, sharp, pungent; harsh, vindictive

598 πλούσιος — rich, wealthy
• Opp.: πένης[717]
• Cf. vb πλουτεῖν[1265], n. πλοῦτος[92]

599 πολέμιος — hostile, οἱ πολέμιοι the enemy, ἡ πολεμία (sc. γῆ) enemy territory
• Opp.: φίλιος[616]
• Cf. vb πολεμεῖν[1267], n. πόλεμος[93]

600 πονηρός — bad: of poor quality; badly behaved, villainous, unscrupulous
• Opp.: χρηστός[542]

601 προτεραῖος — previous, often ἡ προτεραία or ἡ προτεραία ἡμέρα 'the previous day'
• Cf. next; ctr. adj. ὑστεραῖος[613]

602 πρότερος — former, previous, earlier; adv. πρότερον formerly or before that, sooner (+ gen. prior to)
• Opp.: ὕστερος[614]
• Cf. adj. πρῶτος[529]

603 ῥᾴδιος* — easy
• Comp. ῥᾴων, Sup. ῥᾷστος
• Opp.: χαλεπός[540]

604 σκαιός — left: lefthanded, i.e. awkward, gauche, unsophisticated
• Cf. adj. ἀριστερός[556]

605 σκληρός — hard, rigid, stiff; stubborn, harsh, austere

606 σμικρός — Cf. μικρός[587]

607 σπουδαῖος — worth taking seriously: good, excellent, of high/ decent quality
• Opp.: φαῦλος[538]
• Cf. vb σπουδάζειν[1035], n. σπουδή[322]

608 σφαλερός — slippery, perilous, precarious
• Cf. vb σφάλλεσθαι[1134]

609 σφέτερος — their own, their

34

610 τελευταῖος   *last, final;* often used predicatively w. vb, cf. s.
τελευτᾶν[1163]; τὸ τελευταῖον *finally*
• Cf. n. τελευτή[329]

611 τίμιος   *honoured, valued; costly*
• Cf. n. τιμή[331], vb τιμᾶν[1164]

612 ὑμέτερος   *your* (plural reference, cf. under σός[531])

613 ὑστεραῖος   *coming later, next,* ἡ ὑστεραία usually without
ἡμέρα *the next day*
• Opp.: προτεραῖος[601]
• Cf. next

614 ὕστερος   *subsequent, later, too late* (as ὕστεροι
ἀφίκοντο); adv. -ον, -ον οὐ πολλῷ '(very) soon
afterwards', χρόνῳ -ον 'some time later'
• Opp.: πρότερος[602]
• Cf. foregoing

615 φανερός   *conspicuous, visible, clear, apparent*
• Opp.: ἀφανής[679]

616 φίλιος   *friendly* (to: dat.)
• Opp.: πολέμιος[599]
• Cf. adj. φίλος[539], vb φιλεῖν[1283], n. φιλία[253]

617 φοβερός   *inspiring fear, frightening, formidable; full of
fear, fearful*
• Cf. vb φοβεῖσθαι[1312], n. φόβος[116]

618 ψυχρός   *cold*
• Opp.: θερμός[501]

A.1.c Contracted types -ΟΥΣ -Η -ΟΥΝ

619 ἁπλοῦς   *single, simple, straightforward;* adv. ἁπλῶς
simply, absolutely

620 διπλοῦς   *twofold, double*

A.1.d -ΟΣ with fem. -ΕΙΑ [cf. C below]

621 πρᾷος πραεῖα πρᾷον   *mild, mild-mannered, gentle, placid*

A.2.a -ΟΣ: fem. -ΟΣ, neut. -ΟΝ [entries marked § occasionally fem. in -Η or -Α]

622 ἄγροικος   *living in the country* (see n. ἀγρός[26] and vb
οἰκεῖν[1255]), *rustic: boorish, crude, rude, stupid*
• Opp.: ἀστεῖος[558]

623 ἄδηλος   *unclear, uncertain*
• Opp.: δῆλος[496]

624 ἄδικος — unjust, dishonest, τὸ δίκαιον καὶ τὸ ἄδικον (or in plur.) 'right and wrong'
• Opp.: δίκαιος⁵⁶⁷
• Cf. vb ἀδικεῖν¹¹⁸², n. ἀδίκημα⁴⁵⁵, ἀδικία¹⁶⁷

625 ἀδύνατος — unable (commonly + inf.), incapable; incapacitated, impotent; impossible, ἀδύνατον or -ατα (ἐστι) + inf., 'it is ... to...'
• Opp.: δυνατός⁴⁹⁷

626 ἀθάνατος§ — undying, immortal, everlasting
• Opp.: θνητός⁵⁰² • Cf. n. θάνατος⁵³

627 ἀκόλαστος — [~ κολάζειν 'punish': 'unpunished' or 'incorrigible'] immoral
• Opp.: σώφρων⁷¹¹

628 ἀκούσιος — involuntary, unintentional, commonly of offences
• Opp.: ἑκούσιος⁵⁶⁸
• Cf. adj. ἄκων⁷¹²

629 ἄκυρος — invalid, unratified
• Opp.: κύριος⁵⁸²

630 ἄλογος — running counter to reason: irrational, absurd, unexpected
• Cf. n. λόγος⁷¹, adj. εὔλογος⁶⁵¹

631 ἀναίτιος — not responsible (for: gen.)
• Opp.: αἴτιος⁵⁴⁹

632 ἀνάξιος§ — unworthy, undeserving (of: gen.)
• Opp.: ἄξιος⁵⁵⁵

633 ἀνόσιος — unholy, unrighteous, as not being sanctioned by the gods
• Opp.: ὅσιος⁵⁹³

634 ἀξιόλογος — worth mentioning, remarkable, notable
• Cf. adj. ἄξιος⁵⁵⁵, n. λόγος⁷¹

635 ἄπειρος — inexperienced, ignorant (in/ of: gen.)
• Opp.: ἔμπειρος⁶⁴⁷
• Cf. n. ἀπειρία¹⁷⁵

636 ἄπιστος — mistrustful; untrustworthy, incredible
• Opp.: πιστός⁵²⁷
• Cf. vb ἀπιστεῖν¹¹⁹⁵, n. ἀπιστία¹⁷⁶

637 ἄπορος — impassable; difficult to cope with/ deal with, impracticable; without resources, needy
• Opp.: εὔπορος⁶⁵²
• Cf. vb ἀπορεῖν¹¹⁹⁷, n. ἀπορία¹⁷⁹

638 ἄπρακτος — not achieving one's object, unsuccessful
• Cf. vb πράττειν[1023]

639 ἀπροσδόκητος — unexpected, unforeseen
• Cf. vb προσδοκᾶν[1160]

640 ἀργός — not working [i.e. ἀ-εργός: ἔργον[396]], idle, lazy

641 ἄτιμος — dishonoured, esp. deprived of civic rights, disfranchised
• Cf. vb ἀτιμοῦν[1315], n. ἀτιμία[183]

642 ἄτοπος — out of place [τόπος[109]], out of the way, extraordinary, odd, bizarre, absurd

643 αὐτόνομος — autonomous, independent (of individuals, cities etc.)
• Cf. αὐτός[1398], n. νόμος[78]

644 ἄφθονος — ungrudged, plentiful, abundant
• Cf. n. φθόνος[114]

— βάρβαρος — Cf. s. βάρβαρος[36]

645 βέβαιος§ — secure, stable, firm, reliable, certain
• Cf. vb βεβαιοῦν[1316]

646 γνώριμος§ — well known, familiar; as noun, acquaintance

647 ἔμπειρος — experienced, practised, skilled (in: gen.)
• Opp.: ἄπειρος[635]
• Cf. n. ἐμπειρία[194]

648 ἔρημος§ — (persons/ places) deserted, desolate, isolated, solitary, destitute

649 ἕτοιμος§ — ready (to, inf.); to hand, there for the taking, certain, assured
• Cf. vb ἑτοιμάζειν[941]

650 εὐδόκιμος — enjoying a good reputation, celebrated, famous
• Cf. vb εὐδοκιμεῖν[1229]

651 εὔλογος — reasonable, fair
• Cf. n. λόγος[71], adj. ἄλογος[630]

652 εὔπορος — affording easy passage; easily achieved, easy; resourceful; well provided, well off
• Opp.: ἄπορος[637]
• Cf. vb εὐπορεῖν[1231], n. εὐπορία[204]

653 ἥμερος — tame, cultivated; civilised, humane
• Opp.: ἄγριος[545]

654 ἡσύχιος/
655 ἥσυχος — quiet, at rest, inactive

• Cf. vb ἡσυχάζειν[945], n. ἡσυχία[211]

656 μετέωρος — *high in the air, in mid-air; out at sea; in suspense, uncertain, precarious*

657 ὀλίγωρος — *showing little concern, contemptuous, scornful (of: gen.)*
- Cf. vb ὀλιγωρεῖν[1258]

658 πανοῦργος — *tricky, unscrupulous, wicked; clever, smart*

659 παράδοξος — *contrary to expectation, beyond belief (cf. s. n. δόξα[265])*

660 πάτριος§ — *inherited from one's fathers, hereditary,* τὰ πάτρια *ancestral custom, tradition*
- Cf. adj. πατρῷος[596], n. πατήρ[156]

661 πρόθυμος — *enthusiastic, zealous, eager, determined*
- Cf. vb προθυμεῖσθαι[1307], n. προθυμία[240]

662 πρόχειρος — *ready to hand, readily available*

663 ῥᾴθυμος — *easy-going, too easy-going* or *casual, negligent, inert*
- Cf. n. ῥᾳθυμία[242]

664 ταλαίπωρος — *wretched, miserable*
- Cf. vb ταλαιπωρεῖν[1278]

665 φιλότιμος* — *loving/ aspiring to honour*
- Cf. n. φιλοτιμία[254]

666 φρόνιμος — *prudent, intelligent*
- Opp.: ἄφρων[708]
- Cf. n. φρόνησις[364], vb φρονεῖν[1286]

667 ὠφέλιμος§ — *of service, beneficial*
- Cf. vb ὠφελεῖν[1292], n. ὠφελία[260]

A.2.b
Contracted type -ΟΥΣ, fem. -ΟΥΣ, neut. -ΟΥΝ

668 εὔνους — *displaying good will, well-disposed, loyal*
- Cf. n. εὔνοια[203]

B -ΗΣ: fem. -ΗΣ, neut. -ΕΣ

669 ἀδεής — *fearless, secure;* very common: adv. ἀδεῶς
- Cf. n. δέος[423]

670 ἀήθης — *unaccustomed, unused to (gen.)*
- Opp.: συνήθης[692]
- Cf. adj. εὐήθης[684]

671 ἀκριβής — *exact, precise, meticulous, thorough*

672 ἀληθής — *true* (often τἀληθῆ = τὰ ἀληθῆ (tell etc.) *the truth*); *genuine, real* — ὡς ἀληθῶς 'in a true sense, really and truly, in reality'
- Opp.: ψευδής[694]
- Cf. n. ἀλήθεια[171]

673 ἀμαθής — *stupid, ignorant*
- Opp.: σοφός[532]
- Cf. vb μανθάνειν[986]

674 ἀναιδής — *shameless, impudent*
- Cf. n. αἰδώς[366]

675 ἀσεβής — *impious*
- Opp.: εὐσεβής[686]
- Cf. n. ἀσέβεια[180], vb ἀσεβεῖν[1201]

676 ἀσθενής — *weak, ill*
- Opp.: ἰσχυρός[578], ὑγιής[693]
- Cf. n. ἀσθένεια[181], vb ἀσθενεῖν[1202]

677 ἀσφαλής — *safe, secure*
- Cf. n. ἀσφάλεια[182]

678 αὐτάρκης — *self-supporting, independent*
- Cf. αὐτός[1398] and ἀρκεῖν[1200]

679 ἀφανής — *out of sight, unseen, invisible*
- Opp.: φανερός[615]

680 δυστυχής — *unfortunate*
- Opp.: εὐτυχής[687]
- Cf. vb δυστυχεῖν[1216], n. δυστυχία[190]

681 ἐναργής — *distinct, crystal-clear, perspicuous, manifest*

682 ἐνδεής — *lacking, deficient (in), in need (of)* (gen.), *destitute*
- Cf. n. ἔνδεια[195]

683 ἐπιεικής — *reasonable, fair-minded, decent, honest* (cf. χρηστός[542]); adv. -ῶς *fairly, pretty,* ἐ. πάλαι, 'quite a while ago'

684 εὐήθης — *simple-minded, silly, naive*
- Cf. adj. ἀήθης[670], συνήθης[692]

685 εὐμενής — *well-disposed, friendly, favourable*

686 εὐσεβής — *pious, god-fearing*
- Opp.: ἀσεβής[675]
- Cf. n. εὐσέβεια[205], vb εὐσεβεῖν[1232]

687 εὐτυχής — *fortunate, successful*
- Opp.: δυστυχής[680]
- Cf. vb εὐτυχεῖν[1233], n. εὐτυχία[206]

688 πλήρης

full (of: gen.), *fully manned*
- Opp.: κενός[508]
- Cf. vb πληροῦν[1325]

689 σαφής

distinct, clear, plain, obvious

690 συγγενής

akin, as noun *kinsman, relative*
- Cf. n. συγγένεια[246]

691 συνεχής

continuous, continual, unremitting, freq. in adverbial form συνεχῶς

692 συνήθης

habitual, customary; + dat., *habituated, accustomed to; used to, on familiar terms with*
- Opp.: ἀήθης[670]
- Cf. adj. εὐήθης[684]

693 ὑγιής

healthy, sound, wholesome
- Opp.: ἀσθενής[676]
- Cf. vb ὑγιαίνειν[1060]

694 ψευδής

lying, false, untrue
- Opp.: ἀληθής[672]
- Cf. vb ψεύδεσθαι[1139], n. ψεῦδος[453]

C -ΥΣ: fem. -ΕΙΑ, neut. -Υ

695 βαθύς

deep

696 βαρύς

heavy; weighing heavily on one, *onerous, oppressive*

697 βραδύς

slow
- Opp.: ταχύς[706]

698 βραχύς

short, brief, small, few, limited
- Opp.: μακρός[585]

699 εὐρύς

wide, broad
- Opp.: στενός[533] • Cf. n. εὖρος[429]

700 ἡδύς *

sweet
- Comp. ἡδίων, Sup. ἥδιστος
- Cf. vb ἥδεσθαι[1107], n. ἡδονή[297]

701 ἥμισυς

half (noun τὸ ἥμισυ)

702 θῆλυς

female
- Opp.: ἄρρην[713]

703 θρασύς

bold, confident, but more often *over-bold, brazen, insolent*
- Cf. n. θράσος[433]

704 ὀξύς

sharp (to touch, taste), *keen* (sight), *piercing/ high pitched; quick tempered; quick* (off the mark), *expeditious*

705 παχύς — *thick*
   • Opp.: λεπτός[512]

706 ταχύς* — *fast, quick, rapid*
   • Comp. θάττων, Sup. τάχιστος
   • Opp.: βραδύς[697]
   • Cf. n. τάχος[449]

707 τραχύς — *rough, rugged; harsh, severe*

D -ΩΝ: fem. -ΩΝ, neut. -ON, gen. -ΟΝΟΣ

708 ἄφρων — *senseless, foolish, unintelligent*
   • Opp.: φρόνιμος[666]

709 ἐπιστήμων — + gen., *skilled in, possessing specialist knowledge of/ expertise in*
   • Cf. vb ἐπίστασθαι[1382], n. ἐπιστήμη[292]

710 εὐδαίμων — *enjoying (enviable) good fortune, esp. material prosperity*
   • Cf. n. εὐδαιμονία[201]

711 σώφρων — *sensible, prudent; self-controlled, self-disciplined, temperate, chaste*
   • Opp.: ἀκόλαστος[627]
   • Cf. vb σωφρονεῖν[1277], n. σωφροσύνη[327]

E Others

712 ἄκων* [gen. -οντος] -ουσα -ον *unwilling, involuntary*
   • Opp.: ἑκών[714]
   • Cf. adj. ἀκούσιος[628]

713 ἄρρην -εν, gen. -ένος — *male*
   • Opp.: θῆλυς[702]

714 ἑκών -οῦσα -όν — [Cf. under ἄκων[712]] *deliberate(ly), willing(ly), voluntar(il)y*, e.g. ἑκόντες ἐξαπατᾶσθε, 'you're willing to have the wool pulled over your eyes'
   • Cf. adj. ἑκούσιος[568]

715 μέγας* μεγάλη μέγα — *big* etc.
   • Comp. μείζων, Sup. μέγιστος
   • Opp.: μικρός[587]
   • Cf. n. μέγεθος[437]

716 μέλας [gen. -ανος] -αινα -αν — *black, dark*
   • Opp.: λευκός[513]

717 πένης, gen. -ητος — *poor* (also noun *poor person*)
   • Opp.: πλούσιος[598]
   • Cf. n. πενία[233]

[718] πολύς* πολλή πολύ	*much* etc.
	• Comp. πλείων, Sup. πλεῖστος
	• Opp.: ὀλίγος[520]
	• Cf. adv. πολλάκις[842]

F Irregular Comparative/ Superlative

[719] ἀμείνων/	See ἀγαθός[489]
[720] ἄριστος	
[721] βελτίων/	See ἀγαθός[489]
[722] βέλτιστος	
[723] ἐλάττων	Cf. under μικρός[587] and ὀλίγος[520]
[724] ἐλάχιστος	See μικρός[587]
[725] ἥττων/	See κακός[506]
	• Cf. vb ἥττασθαι[1172]
— [ἥκιστος	See adv. ἥκιστα[794]]
[726] θάττων	See ταχύς[706]
[727] κρείττων/	See ἀγαθός[489]
[728] κράτιστος	
	• Cf. vb κρατεῖν[1245], n. κράτος[436]
[729] μείζων/	See μέγας[715]
[730] μέγιστος	
[731] πλείων/	See πολύς[718]
[732] πλεῖστος	
	• Cf. vb πλεονεκτεῖν[1264], n. πλεονεξία[235]
[733] τάχιστος	See τάχυς[706]
[734] χείρων/	See κακός[506]
[735] χείριστος	

III. ADVERBS AND PREPOSITIONS

Only one or two of the adverbs regularly formed from adjectives, as ἀδίκως βραδέως, are included here. Relative adverbs, as ᾗ, ὅθεν, and indefinite adverbs with matching interrogatives, will be found in section V. Many of the adverbs listed here can be used with the gen. or dat., i.e. with prepositional force.

736 ἄγαν		*too much, too*
		• Cf. adv. λίαν[799]
737 ἀεί*		*always*
738 ἄλλη		*in/ to another place, elsewhere; otherwise*
739 ἄλλοθεν		*from elsewhere*
740 ἄλλοθι		*elsewhere*
741 ἄλλοσε		*to another place, in another direction*
742 ἄλλως*		*otherwise*
		• Cf. ἄλλος[1391]
743 ἅμα*		*at the same time*
744 ἀμφοτέρωθεν		*from/ on both sides*
		• Cf. ἀμφότεροι[1392]
745 ἀνά		+ acc., *up, up along, throughout, in groups (etc.) of/ at the rate of*
746 ἄνευ		+ gen., *without* (knowledge, consent, help of); *apart from, besides*
		• Opp.: σύν[852]
747 ἀντί		+ gen., *in place of, in return for*
748 ἄνω		*up, upwards, upstairs;* ἄνω καὶ κάτω (turn etc.) *upside-down*
		• Opp.: κάτω[797]
749 ἅπαξ		*once, on a single occasion*
750 ἀπό		+ gen., *(away) from; following on from, after; as a result of*
751 ἄρτι		*just now, just*
752 αὖ		*in turn,* δ' αὖ *often answering to* μέν[1433], *and on the other hand; in argument, again, next*
753 αὖθις		*again, in turn; hereafter, in future*
754 αὔριον		*tomorrow*
755 αὐτίκα		*immediately, right away; for instance*
756 αὐτόθεν		*from the very (this/ that particular) place*

757 αὐτόθι	*right there, on the spot*
758 αὐτοῦ	*in the very (this/ that very/ particular) place, right here/ there*
759 δεῦρο	*here*, where movement to is in question, *over here, this way*
760 διά	+ acc., *because of, through;* + gen., *across, through, by means of* • Cf. διό¹⁴⁰⁶ (δι' ὅ)
761 διαφερόντως	*differently from,* + gen.; *to an exceptional degree,* + gen. 'as compared with', i.e. *to a greater degree than ...* • Cf. vb διαφέρειν⁹⁰⁹
762 δίς	*twice*
763 ἐγγύς	*near, in the vicinity* (of: gen.)
764 εἰκότως	*reasonably, naturally, not surprisingly, as was to be expected* • Cf. vb ἐοικέναι¹³⁷⁶
765 εἰς	+ acc., *into, on to, up to, in respect of/ in relation to, for the purpose of*
766 εἴσω	*to within, into, inside* (also + gen.) • Opp.: ἔξω⁷⁸⁶
767 εἶτα	*then, then again, next, and then* (w. or without prior καί in incredulous/ indignant questions/ exclamations), *and so, and despite that* • Cf. adv. ἔπειτα⁷⁸⁷
768 ἐκ/ ἐξ	(ἐξ before a vowel) + gen., *out of, from, arising from, after, in accordance with*
769 ἑκάστοτε	*on each occasion, invariably, regularly* • Cf. ἕκαστος¹⁴¹⁵
770 ἐκεῖ	*there*
771 ἐκεῖθεν	*from there*
772 ἐκεῖσε	*there*, where motion to is in question
773 ἐκποδών	*out of the/ one's way* (sts with dat.) • Opp.: ἐμποδών⁷⁷⁵
774 ἐκτός	*outside, out of range;* + gen., *outside of, clear of, exempt from* • Opp.: ἐντός⁷⁸⁴
775 ἐμποδών	*in one's path, presenting an obstacle* (sts with dat.) • Opp.: ἐκποδών⁷⁷³
776 ἐν	+ dat., *in, on, at, in the course of, among/ before*

777 ἔνδον	*inside, within, indoors* (also + gen.)
778 ἕνεκα	+ gen. (commonly postp.), *for the sake of, because of*
779 ἐνθάδε	*here*
780 ἐνθένδε	*from this place/ point*
781 ἐνίοτε	*sometimes*
	• Cf. ἔνιοι[1419]
782 ἐνταῦθα	*here, hereupon, at this point*
783 ἐντεῦθεν	*from here, henceforth*
784 ἐντός	*inside, within* (also + gen.)
	• Opp.: ἐκτός[774]
— ἐξ	See ἐκ[768]
785 ἐξαίφνης	*all of a sudden*
786 ἔξω	*outside, out, out of range* (also + gen.)
	• Opp.: εἴσω[766]
787 ἔπειτα	*then, next, secondly* (commonly just ἔπειτα after a πρῶτον μέν), cf. under εἶτα[767]
788 ἐπί*	See Supp.
789 ἐπίτηδες	*deliberately, on purpose*
790 ἔτι*	*still*
	• Cf. οὐκέτι[824]
791 εὖ	Adv. of ἀγαθός[489], *well, skilfully, properly, soundly, duly, fortunately,* etc.
792 εὐθύς	(or εὐθέως) *at once, directly, immediately*
793 ἤδη	*by now/ then, already; then (and only then); now, right now, instantly, actually now; from now/ then on, from this/ that point*
794 ἥκιστα	(Sup.) *least,* in reply *certainly not;* οὐχ ἥκιστα *not least, above all*
795 ἴσως	*perhaps, maybe*
	• Cf. adj. ἴσος[504]
796 κατά*	See Supp.
797 κάτω	*down(wards), below, downstairs*
	• Opp.: ἄνω[748], q.v.
798 λάθρᾳ	*by stealth, surreptitiously*
	• Cf. vb λανθάνειν[980]
799 λίαν	*excessively, too much, too*
	• Cf. adv. ἄγαν[736]
800 μάλα/	See μέγας[715](Supplement)
801 μᾶλλον/	
802 μάλιστα	

803	μάτην	*in vain, ineffectually, randomly, to no purpose*
804	μετά	+ acc., *after;* + gen., *along with* (οἱ μετὰ ... *one's companions* or *men*), *on the side of, in cooperation with*
805	μεταξύ	*in the middle, between* (also + gen.); *meanwhile:* + partic., ἐβόα τοῦ ἐναντίου μεταξὺ λέγοντος, 'he started to raise his voice as his opponent was in mid-speech'
806	μή	See οὐ[820]
807	μόγις/	*with effort/ difficulty, scarcely, only just*
808	μόλις	
809	νεωστί	*lately, just now* • Cf. adj. νέος[590]
810	νύκτωρ	*during the night, by night* • Cf. n. νύξ[378]
811	νῦν	*now, at the present time, currently,* νῦν δέ often 'but as things stand', 'but as it is' • Opp.: τότε[859]
812	νυνδή	*just now, a moment ago*
813	οἴκαδε	*homewards, to one's home* • Cf. οἶκος[80] and next
814	οἴκοθεν	*from home*
815	οἴκοι	*at home*
816	ὀλιγάκις	*on few occasions, seldom* • Opp.: πολλάκις[842] • Cf. adj. ὀλίγος[520]
817	ὄντως	*really, actually* • Cf. vb εἶναι[1338]
818	ὄπισθεν	*behind* (also + gen.), *at the back, in the rear* • Cf. next
819	ὀπίσω	*backwards, back again*
820	οὐ	(also οὐκ, οὐχ, οὐχί) *not* — 'Oblique' form μή (+ third person subjv. to give sense 'perhaps, it could be that ...', μὴ τοῦτο ἀληθὲς ᾖ, 'maybe this is true')
821	οὐδαμοῦ	*nowhere* • Opp.: πανταχοῦ[832]
822	οὐδαμῶς	*in no way;* in answers, *by no means*
823	οὐδέποτε	*never* • Cf. ποτε[1480]

824 οὐκέτι
no longer, not thereafter, not after all
• Cf. ἔτι[790]

825 οὔπω
not yet
• Cf. πω[851]

826 οὕτω(ς)
thus, so, in this/ that way, to such an extent
• Cf. οὗτος[1468], and ὧδε[864]

827 ὀψέ
late
• Opp.: πρῴ[849]

828 πάλαι*
some time ago
• Cf. adj. παλαιός[594]

829 πάλιν
again, back again; in argument (καὶ) πάλιν
'(and) again'

830 παντάπασι(ν)
altogether, absolutely (often in reply)

831 πανταχόθεν
from all sides/ quarters; in every way/ respect

832 πανταχοῦ
everywhere
• Opp.: οὐδαμοῦ[821]

833 παντελῶς
completely, entirely

834 πάντως
in every way, absolutely, at all costs, in any
case

835 πάνυ
altogether, very, in answers (commonly in form
πάνυ μὲν οὖν) very much so, certainly; οὐ πάνυ
not quite, not all that or not at all

836 παρά
+ acc., into the presence of, to visit, along, in
comparison with, past, contrary to, in contra-
vention of; + gen., from the presence of, from; +
dat., in the presence of, at the house of, among

837 παράπαν
With article, τὸ π. altogether; with neg.,
οὐ (etc.) τὸ π. not at all, emphatically not

838 παραχρῆμα
on the spot, there and then, right away

839 πέλας
in the (immediate) vicinity, οἱ πέλας close
neighbours
• Cf. adv. πλησίον[841]

840 περί
+ acc., around, (at) round about (time, number),
in relation to/ in the sphere of; + gen. about,
concerning, (valued) at (a price); + dat., round
about, (contention) for/ over

841 πλησίον
close by (also + gen.), οἱ πλησίον near
neighbours
• Cf. adv. πέλας[839]

842 πολλάκις
many times, frequently; sts (usually in

conjunction with 'if') *perhaps*
- Opp.: ὀλιγάκις[816]
- Cf. adj. πολύς[718]

843 πόρρω — *far away, at a distance, too far; + gen., far from, far into* (as πόρρω τῆς νυκτός)

844 πόρρωθεν — *from a distance;* temporal, *from way back*

845 πρίν — *before: formerly, in the past; before this/ that time, before x happens;* as conj., *before* or *until*

846 πρό — *+ gen., in front of, before the time of* (πρὸ τοῦ 'before this time, hitherto'), *in preference to*

847 πρός* — See Supp.

848 πρόσθε(ν) — *before, (to a point) in front* (also + gen.); *formerly, on an earlier occasion*

849 πρῴ — *early*
- Opp.: ὀψέ[827]

850 πρώην — *the day before yesterday; the other day*

851 πω — *yet* (temporal)
- Cf. οὔπω[825]

852 σύν — *+ dat., with, in conjunction with, with the help or by the favour of*

853 σφόδρα — *vehemently, strongly, extremely, exceedingly*

854 σχεδόν — (freq. σχεδόν τι) *almost, practically, just about*

855 τάχα — *perhaps*

856 τέως — *for a time; up to this time*

857 τήμερον — *today*

858 τηνικαῦτα — *at this/ that (particular) time*

859 τότε — *then, at that time,* opp. νῦν[811] (ἐν τῷ τότε sc. χρόνῳ 'on that (previous) occasion'); *in that situation* — τοτὲ μὲν ... τοτὲ δέ 'sometimes ... sometimes', 'at one time ... at another'

860 ὑπέρ — *+ acc., beyond, exceeding, + gen. over, on behalf of,* [like περί[840]] *concerning*

861 ὑπό* — See Supp.

862 χθές — *yesterday*

863 χωρίς — *apart, separately; + gen., apart from*

864 ὧδε — *so, so very; in this/ the following way, as follows, like this*
- Cf. οὕτω(ς)[826]

— ὡς — See under ὡς[1498]

865 ὡσαύτως — *in similar fashion, likewise,* ὡσαύτως ἔχει 'the same holds true'

IV. VERBS

A.1 Infinitive in -ειν

866 ἀγγέλλειν — *deliver a message, announce, report*
- Cpd: ἐπ-933 παρ-1008
- Cf. n. ἀγγελία165, ἄγγελος25

867 ἄγειν* — *lead, conduct, etc.*
- Cpd: δι-906; ἀν-άγεσθαι1083

868 ἀγείρειν — *gather together, collect* (not to be confused with ἐγείρειν916, q.v.)
- Cf. vb ἀθροίζειν870

869 ᾄδειν — *sing,* with or without acc.
- Cf. n. ᾠδή341

870 ἀθροίζειν — *gather together, collect, muster*
- Cf. adj. ἀθρόος547, and vb ἀγείρειν868

871 αἴρειν — *lift up, raise, take up, take away;* intrans., *of expeditions, get under way, break camp;* middle, *take upon oneself, undertake*

872 ἀκούειν* — *hear, listen to*
- Cpd: ὑπ-1061

873 ἁμαρτάνειν — *be wrong, make a mistake, err, commit an offence;* + gen. (opp. τυγχάνειν1057), *miss, fail to achieve*
- Cf. n. ἁμάρτημα457, ἁμαρτία172

874 ἀνα-βαίνειν — *go up/ upstairs, mount, embark; go* from coast *inland*
- Opp.: καταβαίνειν956

875 ἀνα-γιγνώσκειν — *read out, read*

876 ἀναγκάζειν — *coerce, compel,* + acc. (and inf.)
- Cf. adj. ἀναγκαῖος553, n. ἀνάγκη272

877 ἀναλίσκειν — *use up, spend*

878 ἀνδραποδίζειν — *enslave, sell into slavery*
- Cf. n. ἀνδράποδον386

879 ἀντ-έχειν — Intrans., *hold out, stick it out, hold one's ground, stand firm*

880 ἀντι-λέγειν — *speak in opposition, offer a counter-argument;* + dat., *argue against, contradict,* + ὡς clause *say by way of reply/ an objection that ...*

881 ἀπ-αγορεύειν   (aor. is ἀπ-ειπεῖν) *forbid, veto,* + dat. and μή and inf., ἀπαγορεύουσί μοι μὴ ποιεῖν ταῦτα, 'they forbid me to do this'

882 ἀπ-έχειν   Intrans., *be distant from* (gen.); middle, + gen., *refrain from, abstain from*

883 ἀπο-βαίνειν   *disembark; result, turn out, come true* (cf. ἐκ-βαίνειν[921])

884 ἀπο-βάλλειν   *throw away, forfeit; lose*

885 ἀπο-διδράσκειν   *run away* (as a runaway slave, δραπέτης)

886 ἀπο-θνῄσκειν   (n.b. perf. τέθνηκα) *die, be killed, executed* (freq. + ὑπό and gen.)
- Opp.: ζῆν[1167]

887 ἀπο-κτείνειν   *kill, put to death, execute* (*be killed* see foreg.)

888 ἀπο-λαύειν   *enjoy an advantage,* + gen. *have the benefit of, derive enjoyment from*

889 ἀπο-στέλλειν   *send off, dispatch*
- Cf. vb ἐπι-[937]

890 ἀρέσκειν   *please, satisfy, be congenial to,* + dat. person

891 ἁρπάζειν   *snatch, seize, plunder*

892 ἄρχειν*   *rule; begin*
- Cpd: ὑπ-[1062]
- Cf. adj. ἀρχαῖος[557], n. ἀρχή[274], ἄρχων[136]

893 ἀτιμάζειν   *dishonour, show no respect for*
- Opp.: τιμᾶν[1164]
- Cf. vb ἀτιμοῦν[1315]

894 αὐξάνειν/ αὔξειν   *increase, augment, strengthen,* pass. *grow (in stature), increase*

895 βαδίζειν   *go on foot, walk, march*

896 βαίνειν   *go, make one's way, march, advance* [note also causal βιβάζειν *make to go* etc.]
- Cpd: ἀνα-[874] ἀπο-[883] δια-[904] ἐκ-[921] κατα-[956] παρα-[1007] συμ-[1042]

897 βάλλειν   *throw, cast; hit, pelt one with a missile* (dat.)
- Cpd: ἀπο-[884] δια-[905] εἰσ-[920] ἐκ-[922] μετα-[991] προσ-[1026]
- Cf. n. βέλος[421]

898 βλάπτειν   *damage, hurt, injure*
- Cf. adj. βλαβερός[560], n. βλάβη[277]

899 βλέπειν   *look in a certain direction*

900 γιγνώσκειν*   *get to know* etc.
- Opp.: ἀγνοεῖν[1181]

901 γράφειν
- Cpd: ἀνα-875 κατα-957 μετα-992 συγ-1038
write, or *formally propose, draft* measure;
middle, *indict* (aor. pass. γραφῆναι *be indicted*)
- Cpd: συγ-1039
- Cf. n. γράμμα458, γραφή282

902 δακρύειν
shed tears
- Cf. n. δάκρυον390

903 δανείζειν
lend, middle *borrow*

904 δια-βαίνειν
cross, traverse

905 δια-βάλλειν
set at odds; slander, misrepresent, (seek to)
discredit
- Cf. n. διαβολή284

906 δι-άγειν
pass, spend time (e.g. τὸν βίον); *without*
object, pass time or *delay*

907 δια-μέλλειν
delay, be dilatory

908 δια-τρίβειν
spend (often χρόνον δ.)/ *waste time, be busy,*
occupied
- Cf. n. διατριβή285

909 δια-φέρειν
be different from or *surpass* (gen., cf. adv.
διαφερόντως761); *often impers.,* οὐδὲν
διαφέρει, 'it makes no difference' — Middle,
differ with, be at odds with, *quarrel* with (dat.)

910 δια-φθείρειν
destroy, eliminate, ruin, spoil; corrupt a person

911 διδάσκειν*
teach
- Cf. n. διδάσκαλος43

912 δικάζειν
act as juror, give a judgement, δίκην δικάζειν
deliver legal judgement or *verdict;* middle, w.
or without δίκην, *go to law* with one (dat.)
- Cf. n. δικαστήριον394, δικαστής3

913 διώκειν
chase, pursue (also *pursue* an object, e.g. τὴν
ἀλήθειαν); *prosecute*

914 δοξάζειν
suppose, imagine (that, acc. and inf.); *hold an*
opinion (δόξας δ. *entertain opinions*)
- Cf. n. δόξα265

915 δουλεύειν
be a slave; + dat., *be a slave to, subject to*
- Cf. n. δουλεία189, δοῦλος44, vb δουλοῦν1319

916 ἐγείρειν
awaken, rouse (not to be confused with
ἀγείρειν868, q.v.)

917 ἐθέλειν
(also θέλειν) *wish, want, be willing, consent*
(with neg. in aor. *refuse* (outright)), + inf.
- Cf. vb βούλεσθαι1093

51

918 εἰκάζειν	*liken, compare; conjecture*
919 εἴργειν	*shut in/ out, imprison, exclude, check, block;* + inf., *hinder /inhibit* from doing
920 εἰσ-βάλλειν	+ εἰς and acc., *invade* • Cf. n. εἰσβολή²⁹⁰
921 ἐκ-βαίνειν	*go/ get out of* (ἐκ + gen., or gen. alone); *turn out, come true* (cf. ἀπο-βαίνειν⁸⁸³)
922 ἐκ-βάλλειν	*throw out, jettison, expel, banish*
923 ἐκ-πίπτειν	*fall out, be thrown out, expelled, banished*
924 ἐκ-πλήττειν	*strike with panic, alarm, consternation, severely shock* • Cf. n. ἔκπληξις³⁵¹
925 ἐλαύνειν	*drive, ride* (w. or without object), *press on, march; plague, harass* a person • Cpd: ἐξ-⁹³¹
926 ἐλέγχειν	*put to the test, subject to cross-examination, (attempt to) disprove/ refute*
927 ἕλκειν	*drag, draw*
928 ἐλπίζειν	*expect, hope,* freq. with fut. inf., as ἐλπίζετε φεύξεσθαι, 'you are hoping to escape' • Cf. n. ἐλπίς³⁷¹
929 ἐμ-μένειν	*stay in* a place (ἐν + dat.); + dat., *abide by, stand by, hold to;* without case, *hold good, remain in force* • Opp.: παρα-βαίνειν¹⁰⁰⁷
930 ἐμ-πίπτειν	+ dat., *fall upon, take (sudden) possession of,* of uncontrollable urges etc.
931 ἐξ-ελαύνειν	*drive out, expel, banish*
932 ἐξετάζειν	*examine closely, scrutinize, review*
933 ἐπ-αγγέλλειν	*issue orders;* in middle, *offer freely* (+ acc., or inf., to do), or *profess* (+ acc., or inf.)
934 ἐπ-αμύνειν	+ dat., *render assistance to, succour* • Cf. vb ἀμύνεσθαι¹⁰⁸²
935 ἐπ-έχειν	*stop, keep in check;* without case, *stop, cease* (from: gen.)
936 ἐπι-βουλεύειν	*plot/ intrigue against, have designs on* (+ dat.)
937 ἐπι-στέλλειν	*send a (written) message; issue instructions* (to one: dat.) • Cf. vb ἀπο-⁸⁸⁹, and n. ἐπιστολή²⁹³
938 ἐπι-τηδεύειν	*actively pursue, practise* (occupation, mode of

	conduct etc.)
	• Cf. adj. ἐπιτήδειος⁵⁷¹, n. ἐπιτήδευμα⁴⁶⁰
939 ἐπι-τρέπειν	*entrust, turn over to*
940 ἐσθίειν	*eat*
941 ἑτοιμάζειν	(also middle) *prepare, get ready*, + acc.
	• Cf. adj. ἑτοῖμος⁶⁴⁹
942 εὑρίσκειν	*find, devise, gain, get*
943 ἔχειν*	*have, possess* etc.
	• Cpd: ἀντ-⁸⁷⁹ ἀπ-⁸⁸² ἐπ-⁹³⁵ κατ-⁹⁶³ μετ-⁹⁹⁴ παρ-¹⁰¹¹ προ-¹⁰³¹ προσ-¹⁰²⁷; ἀν-έχεσθαι¹⁰⁸⁵
944 ἥκειν	*have come,* often *have come back, returned*
	• Cpd: προσ-¹⁰²⁸
945 ἡσυχάζειν	*be at rest, inactive* (often in military context)
	• Cf. n. ἡσυχία²¹¹, adj. ἡσύχιος⁶⁵⁴/ ἥσυχος⁶⁵⁵
946 θάπτειν	*bury, inter*
947 θαυμάζειν	*be surprised, marvel,* commonly + εἰ, 'that'; + acc. (sts gen.), *marvel at, admire*
	• Cf. adj. θαυμάσιος⁵⁷⁴, θαυμαστός⁵⁰⁰
— θέλειν	See ἐθέλειν⁹¹⁷
948 θεραπεύειν	*treat medically; take care of, look after, attend carefully to; act like a servant of, flatter*
949 θύειν	*sacrifice, offer* (victim to gods)
	• Cf. n. θυσία²¹⁴
950 ἱκετεύειν	*supplicate, beseech*
	• Cf. n. ἱκέτης⁹
951 ἰσχύειν	*be strong, powerful, have force* or *validity*
	• Cf. adj. ἰσχυρός⁵⁷⁸, n. ἰσχύς³⁷⁵
— κάειν	See καίειν⁹⁵⁴
952 καθαίρειν	*cleanse, purge, purify*
	• Cf. adj. καθαρός⁵⁷⁹
953 καθ-εύδειν	*lie down to sleep, go to bed, sleep*
954 καίειν/ κάειν	*consume with fire, burn;* pass., *burn, be on fire*
	• Cpd: κατα-⁹⁵⁸
955 κάμνειν	*toil, be tired, ill/ an invalid, afflicted*
956 κατα-βαίνειν	*go down/ downstairs, descend; go from interior to coast* (or *from city to port*)
	• Opp.: ἀνα-βαίνειν⁸⁷⁴
957 κατα-γιγνώσκειν	*bring a charge of* (acc.) *against* (gen.), or *pass a sentence of* (acc.) *on* (gen.), *convict* one *of*
958 κατα-καίειν	*burn down, to the ground*

959 κατα-λαμβάνειν — *seize, occupy; befall, overtake; find* on arrival, *come upon*

960 κατα-λείπειν — *leave behind, abandon; bequeath*

961 κατα-λύειν — *break up, dissolve, bring to an end*

962 κατα-φεύγειν — *flee for refuge/ protection*

963 κατ-έχειν — *restrain, control, master, possess, occupy*

964 κελεύειν — *urge, instruct, tell ... to, recommend* or *stipulate that one should,* + (acc. and) inf.
  • Cf. vb παρα-κελεύεσθαι[1124]

965 κερδαίνειν — *gain, derive profit*
  • Cf. n. κέρδος[435]

966 κηρύττειν — *make/ issue a proclamation*
  • Cf. n. κῆρυξ[147]

967 κινδυνεύειν — *be in/ incur danger, run a risk* (often κίνδυνον[63] κ.; of -ing, inf.); also expresses likelihood, as κινδυνεύεις πράγματ᾽ ἔχειν, 'it looks as if you are/ you are possibly in trouble'

968 κλάειν/ κλαίειν — *cry, weep,* often *be sorry, regret it*

969 κλείειν — *shut, close, block*

970 κλέπτειν — *steal*
  • Cf. n. κλέπτης[10], κλοπή[299]

971 κολάζειν — *chastise, punish*
  • Cf. adj. ἀκόλαστος[627]

972 κολακεύειν — *be a flatterer,* + acc., *flatter*
  • Cf. n. κολακεία[217], κόλαξ[148]

973 κομίζειν — *convey, bring, conduct;* middle, *get back, recover, acquire;* middle/ pass., *get oneself back, get back*

974 κόπτειν — *cut (down), strike, knock about, knock on* (door)

975 κρίνειν — *judge, decide on; put on trial*
  • Cpd: ἀπο-κρίνεσθαι[1088]

976 κρύπτειν — *hide, conceal*

977 κωλύειν — *prevent, hinder* (from -ing: inf.)

978 λαγχάνειν — *obtain by lot;* λ. δίκην *bring* action/ suit (against: dat.)

979 λαμβάνειν — *take* (often *take in marriage*), *get, receive, be given, apprehend, understand;* middle, + gen., *take hold of, grip*
  • Cpd: κατα-[959] συλ-[1040] ὑπο-[1064]

980 λανθάνειν   *escape (the) notice* (of: acc.), + part., ἐλάθομέν σε φυγόντες, 'we got away before you noticed/ before you realised what was going on'
- Cpd: ἐπι-λανθάνεσθαι[1103]
- Cf. adv. λάθρᾳ[798]

981 λέγειν*   *speak* etc.
- Cpd: ἀντι-[880] συλ-[1041]; δια-λέγεσθαι[1098]
- Cf. n. λόγος[71]

982 λείπειν   *leave, leave behind*
- Cpd: κατα-[960] παρα-[1009]
- Cf. adj. λοιπός[514]

983 λήγειν   *cease,* + part.; or + gen., from an activity

984 λούειν   *wash,* middle *wash oneself, bathe*

985 λύειν   *loosen, undo, release; dissolve, repeal, annul, break; resolve, solve;* middle, *secure the release of by paying a ransom*
- Cpd: κατα-[960]

986 μανθάνειν   *learn, understand*
- Cf. adj. ἀμαθής[673]

987 μεθύειν   *be intoxicated,* literally or metaphorically

988 μέλειν   Impers., *there is a concern* to (dat.) of/ about (gen.), as μέλει μοι τούτων, 'I'm concerned about this', 'this concerns me/ matters to me'
- Cpd: μετα-μέλειν[993], ἐπι-μέλεσθαι[1104]
- Cf. vb ἀμελεῖν[1118]

989 μέλλειν   *be about* to, *on the point* of, *going* to, *be sure* to, *intend* to, commonly with fut. inf.; *hesitate, delay, be dilatory* — τὰ μέλλοντα *the future*
- Cpd: δια-[907]

990 μένειν   *stay, stay put, remain, wait;* + acc., *wait for*
- Cpd: ἐμ-[929] ὑπο-[1065]

991 μετα-βάλλειν   *alter, change* (also intrans.)
- Cf. n. μεταβολή[306]

992 μετα-γιγνώσκειν   *change one's mind, repent*

993 μετα-μέλειν*   *repent*

994 μετ-έχειν   *have a share in, participate in,* + gen.

995 μηνύειν   *divulge; lay information* against one (κατά + gen.), *denounce*

996 νέμειν   *distribute, allot; hold sway over, possess, inhabit*

997 νεωτερίζειν

engage in revolutionary/ subversive activities
• Cf. adj. νέος⁵⁹⁰

998 νομίζειν

+ acc., *regard/ treat as customary, observe, acknowledge, believe in;* + acc. and inf., *think, believe* that
• Cf. n. νόμος⁷⁸

999 οἰκίζειν

found as a colony, *colonise* a place

1000 οἰκτίρειν

pity
• Cf. n. οἶκτος⁸¹

1001 ὀνειδίζειν

reproach, + dat.
• Cf. n. ὄνειδος⁴⁴²

1002 ὀνομάζειν

name, term, speak the word(s)...
• Cf. n. ὄνομα⁴⁶³

1003 ὁπλίζειν

arm, equip, furnish with (heavy) arms
• Cf. n. ὅπλα⁴⁰⁶, ὁπλῖται¹⁶

1004 ὀφείλειν

owe, have to pay

1005 παιδεύειν

educate
• Cf. n. παιδεία²²⁹

1006 παίζειν

play, jest, joke, fool around, not be serious
• Opp.: σπουδάζειν¹⁰³⁵
• Cf. n. παιδιά²³⁰, παιδίον⁴⁰⁷/ παῖς¹⁵⁵

1007 παρα-βαίνειν

step beyond, transgress, contravene, violate
• Opp.: ἐμ-μένειν⁹²⁹

1008 παρ-αγγέλλειν

transmit messages, send word (to: dat.)

1009 παρα-λείπειν

leave to one side, pass over, omit

1010 παρα-σκευάζειν

prepare, make ready; middle, *get oneself ready, make one's preparations*
• Cf. n. παρασκευή³¹²

1011 παρ-έχειν*

provide, furnish etc.

1012 παρ-οξύνειν

spur on or *incense,* + inf., *provoke* into doing

1013 πάσχειν*

have happen to one, experience etc.
• Cf. n. πάθος⁴⁴⁵

1014 πατάσσειν

strike, strike (one) *a blow*

1015 παύειν

stop, freq. w. acc. + part., γελῶντας παύει τοὺς ἐχθρούς, 'he is stopping his enemies from laughing'; middle, + part., *stop* (i.e. cease from) doing

1016 πείθειν

persuade, talk round; middle, + dat., *listen to one, do as one says, obey* [opp.: ἀπειθεῖν¹¹⁹³]; perf. πέπεισμαι *trust, be convinced* (by: dat.)
• Cf. adj. πιθανός⁵²⁶

1017 πέμπειν	*send, escort* • Cpd: μετα-πέμπεσθαι[1119]
1018 πιέζειν	*press tight, squeeze, exert severe pressure on, oppress*
1019 πίνειν	*drink*
1020 πίπτειν	*fall, throw oneself, be thrown* • Cpd: ἐκ-[923] ἐμ-[930] προσ-[1029]
1021 πιστεύειν	*believe in, trust,* + dat.; + acc. and inf., *believe, be confident* that • Opp.: ἀπιστεῖν[1195] • Cf. n. πίστις[353], adj. πιστός[527]
1022 πορίζειν	*furnish, provide;* middle, *procure* • Cf. n. πόρος[96]
1023 πράττειν*	*carry out* etc. • Cpd: δια-πράττεσθαι[1099] • Cf. n. πρᾶγμα[467], πρᾶξις[356]; adj. ἄπρακτος[638]
1024 πρέπειν	Impers. πρέπει, *it is proper, fitting,* + dat. and inf.
1025 πρεσβεύειν	*serve as ambassador;* in middle, *send ambassadors* • Cf. n. πρεσβεία[238], πρέσβεις[159]
— προ-έχειν	See προύχειν[1031]
1026 προσ-βάλλειν	*mount an attack* (on: dat.) • Cf. n. προσβολή[314]
1027 προσ-έχειν	*apply;* cf. under νοῦς[127]
1028 προσ-ήκειν*	*be appropriate* etc.
1029 προσ-πίπτειν	+ dat., *fall upon, launch an attack on; fall in with, encounter,* of accidents etc. *befall*
1030 προσ-τάττειν	*prescribe, assign, impose* a task on one (dat.); also w. dat. and inf., *direct* one to do, or w. acc. and inf., *stipulate that ... should ...*
1031 προύχειν	(i.e. προ-έχειν) Intrans., *jut out, project; be superior, surpass,* commonly + gen.
1032 ῥίπτειν	*throw, cast, fling*
1033 σημαίνειν	*give a sign/ signal; indicate, signify, mean* • Cf. n. σημεῖον[411]
1034 σπεύδειν	*promote enthusiastically, strive for energetically;* intrans., *be keen, strive energetically, make a determined effort*
1035 σπουδάζειν	*make a determined effort, be serious or earnest;*

+ acc., *be earnest about, pursue zealously*
- Opp.: παίζειν[1006]
- Cf. n. σπουδή[322], adj. σπουδαῖος[607]

1036 στασιάζειν — *form a faction, engage in/ be torn by factional strife*
- Cf. n. στάσις[359]

1037 στρέφειν — *turn, twist*
- Cpd: κατα-στρέφεσθαι[1110]

1038 συγ-γιγνώσκειν — *forgive, pardon*, + dat.
- Cf. n. συγγνώμη[324]

1039 συγ-γράφειν — *compile, compose* (in prose: ctr. ποιεῖν[1266])

1040 συλ-λαμβάνειν — *apprehend, arrest; comprehend, grasp*

1041 συλ-λέγειν — *gather together, collect*

1042 συμ-βαίνειν* — *fit, agree, happen*

1043 συμ-βουλεύειν — + dat. *advise*, in middle *consult*
- Cf. n. σύμβουλος[106]

1044 συμ-φέρειν — *be of advantage, in one's interest*, impers. + dat. and inf., συνήνεγκεν ὑμῖν ἅπαντας ζημιῶσαι, 'it was in your interest to penalise all of them'
- Cf. n. συμφορά[248]

1045 σχολάζειν — *have spare time, be at leisure, have nothing to do; devote one's time/ oneself* to a person or activity (dat.)
- Cf. n. σχολή[326]

1046 σώζειν — *save, preserve; bring safely* to a place (middle/ pass. *arrive safely* at a place)
- Opp.: ἀπολλύναι[1333]
- Cf. n. σωτήρ[161], σωτηρία[250]

1047 ταράττειν — *stir up, throw into confusion* or *disorder, convulse, disrupt*
- Cf. n. ταραχή[328]

1048 τάττειν — *station, post* (in middle *take up battle positions*), *appoint, prescribe, fix, assess* (in perf. part. pass. *fixed, settled, prescribed*)
- Cpd: προσ-[1030]
- Cf. n. τάξις[361]

1049 τείνειν — *stretch, pull tight;* intrans., *stretch out, extend,* with prep. (ἐπί, εἰς, πρός + acc.) *extend to, refer to, be relevant to*

1050 τειχίζειν — *build a wall;* + acc., *fortify, wall*
- Cf. n. τείχισμα[473], τεῖχος[450]

1051 τέμνειν	cut, sever, cut down, often ravage, devastate
1052 τίκτειν	beget/ give birth to, generate, produce
1053 τιτρώσκειν	wound, disable, cripple
1054 τρέπειν	turn, direct; put to flight, rout — Middle/ pass., turn oneself, betake oneself; be turned, face a certain direction
	• Cpd: ἐπι-939
	• Cf. n. τροπή332
1055 τρέφειν	nourish, rear, bring up, support
	• Cf. n. τροφή333
1056 τρέχειν	run
1057 τυγχάνειν*	hit the mark, happen to etc.
	• Cf. n. τύχη334
1058 τύπτειν	beat, give one a beating, strike
1059 ὑβρίζειν	treat hybristically, see s. n. ὕβρις362
1060 ὑγιαίνειν	be healthy; be of sound mind
	• Opp.: ἀσθενεῖν1202
	• Cf. adj. ὑγιής693
1061 ὑπ-ακούειν	respond, answer, comply; respond to, comply with (+ dat.); also + gen., listen to, take notice of
1062 ὑπ-άρχειν	be available, at one's disposal, already here/ there
1063 ὑπ-είκειν	yield, submit, give way (to/ before: dat.)
1064 ὑπο-λαμβάνειν	suppose, assume to be the case, usually with acc. and inf.
1065 ὑπο-μένειν	stay behind, stand firm, stand one's ground; + acc., face up to, resist, or submit to any imposition
1066 ὑπ-οπτεύειν	feel suspicion, be suspicious of, suspect; also with acc. and inf.
	• Cf. n. ὑποψία252
1067 φαίνειν	show, reveal; shine; middle, + inf., appear, seem (as φαίνεται ἁμαρτάνειν); but + part.: φαίνεται ἁμαρτάνων, ' he is clearly/ obviously making a mistake'
1068 φάσκειν	affirm, claim, profess, assert, allege, often + acc. and inf.
1069 φέρειν	carry, convey, bring, fetch; produce; bear, suffer. Intrans., lead to a place; imper. φέρε, come now, well now. Middle, carry off, win
	• Cpd: δια-909 συμ-1044

1070 φεύγειν	*run away, escape* (from: acc.)*; be in/ go into exile; be prosecuted* • Cpd: κατα-962 • Cf. n. φυγάς162, φυγή336
1071 φθάνειν	*act before, anticipate,* commonly with part. or acc. and part., as φθήσεταί σε προσβαλών, 'he will attack before you do', or 'he will attack before you can stop him'
1072 φράζειν	*point out, explain*
1073 φροντίζειν	*consider, ponder;* (+ gen.) *pay heed to, give consideration to, be concerned about*
1074 φύειν	*cause to grow, produce;* in perf. πεφυκέναι, *be naturally, be inclined by nature* • Cf. n. φύσις365
1075 φυλάττειν	*watch, guard, maintain, preserve;* middle, *be careful/ cautious, on one's guard* (against: acc.) • Cf. n. φυλακή337, φύλαξ163
1076 χαίρειν	*rejoice, be glad;* χαῖρε χαίρετε *hallo, goodbye* — χαίρειν ἐᾶν *disregard, dismiss, forget about, write off,* cf. s. ἐᾶν1149
1077 ψέγειν	*find fault, criticise, censure* • Cf. n. ψόγος124

A.2/1 Infinitive in -εσθαι
[ἔρχομαι etc. v. ἰέναι and compounds]

1078 ἀγωνίζεσθαι*	*compete* • Cf. n. ἀγών133
1079 αἰσθάνεσθαι*	*perceive, notice, realise*
1080 αἰσχύνεσθαι	*be ashamed,* + acc. or dat., *at something;* + personal acc., *feel shame before, feel reverence/ respect for* • Cf. n. αἰσχύνη270
1081 ἁλίσκεσθαι	*be caught, taken, convicted* (cf. s. αἱρεῖν1185) • Cf. vb ἀν-αλίσκειν877
1082 ἀμύνεσθαι	Middle, *repel, ward off; requite;* without case, *defend oneself* • Cf. vb ἐπ-αμύνειν934
1083 ἀν-άγεσθαι	*put out to sea*
1084 ἀνα-μιμνήσκεσθαι	*remember, recall, recollect* (freq. + acc. or gen.)
1085 ἀν-έχεσθαι	+ part., *patiently endure, submit to:* ἠνείχετο [note double augment] νικῶντα τὸν ἐχθρὸν

ὁρῶν, 'he put up with seeing his enemy victorious'

1086 ἀπ-αλλάττεσθαι   *depart, make oneself scarce;* + gen., *depart from, rid oneself of*

1087 ἀπ-εχθάνεσθαι   *incur hatred, enmity* (of one: dat.)

1088 ἀπο-κρίνεσθαι   *reply, answer*
•Cf. n. ἀπόκρισις³⁴⁹

1089 ἅπτεσθαι   *grasp, lay hold of, come into contact with,* or *engage in, try one's hand at,* + gen.

1090 αὐλίζεσθαι   *take up quarters, encamp*
• Cf. n. αὐλή²⁷⁵

1091 ἄχθεσθαι   *be vexed, upset, take strong objection* (by/ to: dat., or prep., e.g. ἐπί + dat.; or + part.)

1092 βιάζεσθαι   *apply force, force one's way;* w. object, *treat with violence, force, constrain, overpower*
• Cf. n. βία¹⁸⁴, adj. βίαιος⁵⁵⁹

1093 βούλεσθαι*   *be willing, wish, want*
• Cf. vb ἐθέλειν⁹¹⁷

1094 βουλεύεσθαι   *deliberate, discuss;* in aor., *decide, resolve*
• Cf. vb ἐπι-βουλεύειν⁹³⁶, συμ-βουλεύειν/ -εσθαι¹⁰⁴³, and n. βουλή²⁷⁹

1095 γίγνεσθαι*   *come into being, become, (prove to) be* etc.
• Cpd: ἐπι-¹¹⁰² περι-¹¹²⁵ συγ-¹¹³³

1096 γυμνάζεσθαι   *train/ exercise* (oneself)
• Cf. n. γυμνάσιον³⁸⁹, adj. γυμνός⁴⁹³

1097 δέχεσθαι   *receive, accept, welcome, entertain*
• Cpd: προσ-¹¹²⁸

1098 δια-λέγεσθαι   *converse, engage in conversation/ a dialogue* (with: dat.)

1099 δια-πράττεσθαι   *carry through, execute;* without object, *gain one's ends, achieve one's objectives*

1100 ἐπείγεσθαι   *make haste, press on*

1101 ἕπεσθαι   *follow, accompany, comply with* (+ dat.)

1102 ἐπι-γίγνεσθαι   *come after, next* (τῇ ἐπιγιγνομένῃ ἡμέρᾳ *the following day,* οἱ ἐπιγιγνόμενοι *posterity, descendants*); *come on suddenly* (as storm etc.); + dat., *fall upon, assault*

1103 ἐπι-λανθάνεσθαι   *forget,* + gen.

1104 ἐπι-μέλεσθαι   See ἐπι-μελεῖσθαι¹³⁰²

1105 ἐργάζεσθαι	*perform (manual) labour, work; manufacture, execute, perform,* often with double acc. (cf. s. δίκαιος⁵⁶⁷) • Cf. n. ἔργον³⁹⁶
1106 εὔχεσθαι	*pray* • Cf. n. εὐχή²⁹⁵
1107 ἥδεσθαι	*take pleasure, be delighted* (in/ at: dat.), often with part., *enjoy/ love* doing • Cf. n. ἡδονή²⁹⁷, adj. ἡδύς⁷⁰⁰
1108 ἰσχυρίζεσθαι	*maintain vigorously, insist firmly* (acc. and inf.; or ὅτι/ ὡς) • Cf. adj. ἰσχυρός⁵⁷⁸
1109 καθ-έζεσθαι	*sit down*
1110 κατα-στρέφεσθαι	*subdue, subjugate*
1111 κήδεσθαι	*care deeply about, concern oneself with,* + gen.
1112 λῄζεσθαι	*plunder, ravage* • Cf. n. λῃστής¹²
1113 λογίζεσθαι	*calculate, reckon, infer,* often + acc. and inf. • Cf. n. λογισμός⁷⁰
1114 μαίνεσθαι	*be mad, be out of one's mind* • Cf. n. μανία²¹⁹
1115 μαντεύεσθαι	*consult an oracle* • Cf. n. μαντεῖον⁴⁰¹, μάντις¹⁵¹
1116 μαρτύρεσθαι	*call to witness* • Cf. vb μαρτυρεῖν¹²⁵⁰
1117 μάχεσθαι	*fight* (with: dat.) • Cf. n. μάχη³⁰⁴
1118 μέμφεσθαι	*blame, criticise,* + dat.
1119 μετα-πέμπεσθαι	*send for, summon*
1120 μιμνῄσκεσθαι*	In aor., *mention;* in perf., *remember, recall* • Cpd: ἀνα-¹⁰⁸⁴ • Cf. n. μνήμη³⁰⁸
1121 οἴεσθαι	*think, suppose* (that, (acc. and) inf.) — Common reduced form οἶμαι for οἴομαι, also note crasis ἐγᾦμαι = ἐγὼ οἶμαι
1122 οἴχεσθαι	*have gone, be off; be gone from this world*
1123 ὀργίζεσθαι	*grow/ be angry, furious* (with: dat.) • Cf. n. ὀργή³¹⁰
1124 παρα-κελεύεσθαι	*recommend, encourage,* often + dat.
1125 περι-γίγνεσθαι	*gain superiority, prevail* (over: gen.); *survive, pull through, come out alive; result*

1126 πολιτεύεσθαι   *function as a citizen: take part in government/ politics,* + acc. *administer, govern;* in pass., *be governed*
- Cf. n. πολιτεία[237], πολίτης[18]

1127 πορεύεσθαι   *journey, travel, march, go*

1128 προσ-δέχεσθαι   *accept, admit; await, expect,* often with acc. and fut. inf.

1129 πυνθάνεσθαι   *inquire about* or *ascertain, receive news of,* + acc. or gen.; *hear/ learn* that ...: acc./ gen. and part., or acc. and inf.

1130 σπένδεσθαι   *make a treaty* (with: dat., w. or without object σπονδάς[321])

1131 στρατεύεσθαι   [sts in active] *go on active service, mount/ take part in a military operation/ campaign*
- Cf. n. στρατεία[244] etc.

1132 στρατοπεδεύεσθαι   *make camp, encamp*
- Cf. n. στρατόπεδον[413]

1133 συγ-γίγνεσθαι   + dat., *associate with*

1134 σφάλλεσθαι   *come to grief, suffer a setback, be foiled, disappointed* (+ gen. *be foiled, frustrated in ...*)
- Cf. adj. σφαλερός[608]

1135 τεκμαίρεσθαι   + acc., *make a judgement on, draw conclusions about, infer, estimate* (by/ on the basis of: dat., or ἐκ, ἀπό + gen.)
- Cf. n. τεκμήριον[415]

1136 φείδεσθαι   *be sparing of, use sparingly,* + gen.

1137 φθέγγεσθαι   *utter a sound, open one's mouth;* + acc., *utter*

1138 χαρίζεσθαι   *do a favour, oblige, (seek to) gratify, pander to,* + dat.
- Cf. n. χάρις[383]

1139 ψεύδεσθαι   *lie, tell lies*
- Cf. adj. ψευδής[694], n. ψεῦδος[453]

1140 ψηφίζεσθαι   *vote* (for something: acc.); + (acc. and) inf. *vote to/ that ... should ...*
- Cf. n. ψήφισμα[476], ψῆφος[346]

A.2/2 In aorist only:

1141 ἐρέσθαι   (imperfective [strong] aor., indic. ἠρόμην, fut. ἐρήσεσθαι/ ἐρήσομαι; corresponding pres.: ἐρωτᾶν[1153]) *ask, question, put a question*

VERBS

1142 πρίασθαι	(corresponding pres.: ὠνεῖσθαι1313) *buy, purchase*

B.1 Infinitive in -ᾶν

1143 ἀγαπᾶν — *love, prize; be well content*, often followed up w. εἰ/ ἐάν, 'if', sts with ὅτι, 'that'
• Cf. vb φιλεῖν1283

1144 ἀπ-αντᾶν — *meet, encounter* (one: dat.)

1145 βοᾶν — *shout, bawl, speak in a loud voice*
• Cf. n. βοή278

1146 γελᾶν — *laugh*
• Cpd: κατα-1154
• Cf. adj. γελοῖος561, n. γέλως139

1147 δαπανᾶν — *spend*
• Cf. n. δαπάνη283

1148 δρᾶν — *put into effect, perform, do*
• Opp.: βουλεύεσθαι1094 • Cf. n. δρᾶμα459

1149 ἐᾶν — *allow, permit*, οὐκ ἐᾶν + inf. often *forbid, prohibit, advise against* — With impers. object, *leave be/ alone/ out of the reckoning, drop, forget about*, cf. s. χαίρειν1076

1150 ἐξ-απατᾶν — *deceive, fool, trick, cheat*

1151 ἐπι-τιμᾶν — + dat., *criticise, censure*

1152 ἐρᾶν — *be in love* (with: gen.); + (acc. and) inf., *desire to/ that ... should ...*
• Cf. n. ἐραστής5, ἔρως142

1153 ἐρωτᾶν* — *ask*
• Cf. s. vb ἐρέσθαι1141

1154 κατα-γελᾶν — *laugh to scorn, mock, deride*, often + gen.

1155 μελετᾶν — *study, exercise, practise, rehearse*, without object *study, train*
• Cf. n. μελέτη305

1156 νικᾶν — *be victor, win, prevail*, + acc. *conquer, beat*
• Cf. n. νίκη309

1157 ὁρᾶν — *see;* commonly + part., *see, observe that ...*
• Cpd: περι-1158 προ-1159

1158 περι-ορᾶν — + part. or inf., *watch something happening from the sidelines, sit back and let it happen*, as ταῦτα περιορᾷ γιγνόμενα/ γίγνεσθαι

1159 προ-ορᾶν — *foresee* (also in middle)

1160 προσ-δοκᾶν	have expectations; expect, + acc., or (acc. and) fut./ aor. inf.
	• Cf. adj. ἀπροσδόκητος[639]
1161 σιγᾶν	keep silence, be silent
	• Cf. n. σιγή[318]
1162 σιωπᾶν	be silent, maintain silence
	• Cf. n. σιωπή[319]
1163 τελευτᾶν*	bring to a conclusion, come to an end
	• Cf. adj. τελευταῖος[610], n. τελευτή[329]
1164 τιμᾶν	honour, treat with respect; (active or middle) value, estimate at a price (gen.)
	• Cpd: ἐπι-[1151]
	• Opp.: ἀτιμάζειν[893]/ ἀτιμοῦν[1315]
	• Cf. n. τιμή[331], adj. τίμιος[611]
1165 τολμᾶν	dare, venture, have the courage/ audacity/ nerve to (inf.)
	• Cf. n. τόλμα[267]
1166 φοιτᾶν	go to and fro, (with various preps, e.g. παρά + acc.) visit regularly, call repeatedly on
Cf. also	
1167 ζῆν	(~ ζάω) live, be alive
	• Cf. n. ζῷον[397]

B.2 Infinitive in -ᾶσθαι

1168 αἰτιᾶσθαι	credit with responsibility, charge, accuse (one of an offence: acc. + gen.; also be accused etc. in aor./ perf. pass.); advance as a cause
	• Cf. n. αἰτία[169], adj. αἴτιος[549]
1169 ἀκροᾶσθαι	listen as member of audience; listen to someone (gen.) or something (gen. or acc.)
1170 ἀμιλλᾶσθαι	compete, contend
	• Cf. n. ἅμιλλα[262]
1171 διαιτᾶσθαι	live one's life, live
	• Cf. n. δίαιτα[264]
1172 ἡττᾶσθαι	be inferior (to: gen.), be worsted, beaten (by: ὑπό + gen. or gen. alone), a slave to (e.g. ἡδονῶν[297])
	• Cf. comp. adj. ἥττων[725]
1173 θεᾶσθαι	be a spectator, + acc. look at, view, sts contemplate
	• Cf. n. θεατής[7], θέατρον[398]

65

1174 ἰᾶσθαι	cure, treat medically
	• Cf. n. ἰατρός⁵⁸
1175 κτᾶσθαι	acquire; in perf. κεκτῆσθαι, own, possess
	• Cf. n. κτῆμα⁴⁶¹
1176 μηχανᾶσθαι	construct, contrive, devise, engineer, effect
	• Cf. n. μηχανή³⁰⁷
1177 ὁρμᾶσθαι	rush, charge, swoop; (often with ἐκ) start from a place, as a base ; + inf., rush to, be hell-bent on, have an overwhelming desire to
	• Cf. n ὁρμή³¹¹/ ἀφορμή²⁷⁶
1178 πειρᾶσθαι	make an attempt on, make trial of, test, + gen.; try, attempt, + inf.
	• Cf. n. πεῖρα²³²
Cf. also	
1179 χρῆσθαι*	(~ χράομαι) use
	• Cf. n. χρήματα⁴⁷⁵, adj. χρήσιμος⁵⁴¹

C.1 Infinitive in -εῖν

1180 ἀγανακτεῖν	feel indignation, irritation, annoyance (at: often dat. w. or without ἐπί; or neut. pronoun, τόδε etc.; that: ὅτι or εἰ)
1181 ἀγνοεῖν	not to know, be unaware, ignorant (of: acc.; that: ὅτι or ὡς)
	• Opp.: γιγνώσκειν⁹⁰⁰
1182 ἀδικεῖν*	be dishonest or wrong one
	• Cf. n. ἀδίκημα⁴⁵⁵, ἀδικία¹⁶⁷, adj. ἄδικος⁶²⁴
1183 ἀθρεῖν	observe, consider (+ acc.: a question/ issue)
1184 ἀθυμεῖν	be despondent, dejected, depressed
	• Cf. n. ἀθυμία¹⁶⁸
1185 αἱρεῖν* ~ αἱρεῖσθαι	take, middle choose
	• Cf. under vb ἁλίσκεσθαι¹⁰⁸¹
	• Cpd: -εῖν: ἀν-¹¹⁹⁰ ἀφ-¹²⁰⁵ δι-¹²¹² καθ-¹²³⁸; -εῖσθαι: προ-¹³⁰⁶
1186 αἰτεῖν	ask for (acc.; someone for: two acc.), ask one to (inf.) — NOT ask questions: see ἐρωτᾶν¹¹⁵³ & ἐρέσθαι¹¹⁴¹
	• Cpd: ἀπ-¹¹⁹²
1187 ἀκολουθεῖν	follow, accompany, attend upon (often + dat. person)

66

1188 ἀμελεῖν	(+ gen.) *not care (about), be neglectful* (of) • Opp.: ἐπι-μελεῖσθαι[1302], cf. μέλειν[988] (impers.) • Cf. n. ἀμέλεια[173]
1189 ἀμφισβητεῖν	*dispute, argue*
1190 ἀν-αιρεῖν	*take up* (middle *take up, pick up,* also *shoulder, undertake*); *destroy, wipe out, obliterate, abolish*
1191 ἀνα-χωρεῖν	*withdraw, retreat*
1192 ἀπ-αιτεῖν	*demand back/ the return of*
1193 ἀπειθεῖν	*disobey, refuse to comply with,* + dat. • Opp.: πείθεσθαι[1016]
1194 ἀπειλεῖν	*utter threats against,* + dat.; *threaten to,* + fut. inf.
1195 ἀπιστεῖν	(often + dat.) *be distrustful* (of); *disobey* • Opp.: πιστεύειν[1021] • Cf. n. ἀπιστία[176], adj. ἄπιστος[636]
1196 ἀπο-δημεῖν	*be away from home, out of town/ abroad* • Opp.: ἐπιδημεῖν[1223]
1197 ἀπορεῖν	*be at a loss, perplexed, not know what to do;* + gen., *be in want* or *need of* • Opp.: εὐπορεῖν[1231] • Cf. n. ἀπορία[179], adj. ἄπορος[637]
1198 ἀπο-στερεῖν	*deprive, defraud of,* + double acc. or acc. (person) and gen.
1199 ἀριθμεῖν	*reckon, count up* • Cf. n. ἀριθμός[33]
1200 ἀρκεῖν	*suffice* • Cf. adj. αὐτάρκης[678]
1201 ἀσεβεῖν	*be impious, act impiously* • Opp.: εὐσεβεῖν[1232] • Cf. n. ἀσέβεια[180], adj. ἀσεβής[675]
1202 ἀσθενεῖν	*be weak, ill* (in aor. *fall ill*) • Opp.: ὑγιαίνειν[1060] • Cf. n. ἀσθένεια[181], adj. ἀσθενής[676]
1203 ἀσκεῖν	With or without acc., *train, exercise, practise; cultivate* (virtue etc.)
1204 αὐτομολεῖν	*desert* (from an army) • Cf. n. αὐτόμολος[35]

1205 ἀφ-αιρεῖν	(also middle) *take away from, deprive of,* w. double acc., as ἀφαιρεῖ σε ταῦτα, 'he takes this away from you'
1206 βοηθεῖν	*come/ go to help* or *reinforce, render active assistance to* (dat.) • Cpd: ἐπι-1222 • Cf. n. βοήθεια185
1207 γαμεῖν	*marry,* man as subject, woman as object (acc.); middle, woman as subject, man as object (dat.) • Cf. n. γάμος39
1208 γεωργεῖν	*work on the land* [cf. γῆ280, ἔργον396], *farm,* w. or without acc. • Cf. n. γεωργός40
1209 δεῖν (A)	*put in chains, tie up, imprison*
1210 δεῖν* (B)	Impers., *it is necessary; there is need*
1211 δειπνεῖν	*have dinner, dine* • Cf. n. δεῖπνον391
1212 δι-αιρεῖν	*divide,* in middle *divide among -selves;* active or middle also *distinguish, analyse, determine* (εἰ whether)
1213 δια-τελεῖν	*continue* to do, *carry on* doing, + part., as δια-τελοῦσι πένητες ὄντες, 'they continue to be poor'
1214 δι-οικεῖν	*administer, manage, govern, control*
1215 δοκεῖν*	*seem* etc. • Cf. n. δόξα265, vb δοξάζειν914
1216 δυστυχεῖν	*be unfortunate* • Opp.: εὐτυχεῖν1233 • Cf. adj. δυστυχής680, n. δυστυχία190
1217 δωροδοκεῖν	*take as a bribe, take bribes* • Cf. n. δωροδοκία191
1218 ἐγ-καλεῖν	*bring an accusation* or *charge against* (dat.)
1219 ἐλεεῖν	*pity, show mercy to* • Cf. n. ἔλεος47
1220 ἐν-νοεῖν	*have in mind, reflect upon, consider;* + ὅτι/ ὡς *reflect, bear in mind* that; abs., *understand* • Cf. ἐπι-1225; -εῖσθαι: δια-1298 προ-1308
1221 ἐπ-αινεῖν	*praise, commend* • Cf. παρ-1261, and n. ἔπαινος50
1222 ἐπι-βοηθεῖν	*send a relief force/ reinforcements, intervene militarily* (against: dat.)

1223 ἐπι-δημεῖν — *be at home/ in town*
- Opp.: ἀποδημεῖν[1196]

1224 ἐπι-θυμεῖν — *desire, have a strong wish* (to, for), commonly w. inf. or gen.
- Cf. n. ἐπιθυμία[197]

1225 ἐπι-νοεῖν — *intend, purpose,* often + inf.
- Other compounds: cf. s. ἐννοεῖν[1220]

1226 ἐπι-ορκεῖν — *perjure oneself, commit perjury*
- Cf. n. ὅρκος[87]

1227 ἐπι-σκοπεῖν — *inspect, oversee; meditate, pursue an enquiry*

1228 ἐπι-χειρεῖν — *put one's hand to, take in hand, attempt,* + dat. or inf.

1229 εὐδοκιμεῖν — *enjoy a good reputation, be held in high esteem, be celebrated, popular*
- Cf. adj. εὐδόκιμος[650]

1230 εὐεργετεῖν — *benefit one, do one a good turn*
- Cf. n. εὐεργεσία[202], εὐεργέτης[6]

1231 εὐπορεῖν — *be well supplied or stocked* (with: gen.); *find the means*
- Opp.: ἀπορεῖν[1197]
- Cf. n. εὐπορία[204], adj. εὔπορος[652]

1232 εὐσεβεῖν — *be pious, act piously*
- Opp.: ἀσεβεῖν[1201]
- Cf. n. εὐσέβεια[205], adj. εὐσεβής[686]

1233 εὐτυχεῖν — *be fortunate, successful*
- Opp.: δυστυχεῖν[1216]
- Cf. adj. εὐτυχής[687], n. εὐτυχία[206]

1234 ζητεῖν — *seek, look for, look into, investigate;* + inf., *seek to*

1235 θαρρεῖν/ θαρσεῖν — *have courage, feel confident;* + acc., *face confidently*
- Cf. n. θάρρος/ θάρσος[431]

1236 θεωρεῖν — *view* (games etc.); *contemplate, consider*

1237 θορυβεῖν — *raise a clamour, rumpus* etc. *applaud, boo, heckle,* cf. s. θόρυβος[55]; + acc., *throw into disorder or confusion*

1238 καθ-αιρεῖν — *demolish, destroy, overthrow*

1239 καλεῖν — *call, invite, summon; call by name, term*
- Cpd: ἐγ-[1218] παρα-[1262]

1240 καρτερεῖν — *be patient, endure, persevere*
- Cf. adj. καρτερός[580]

1241 κατα-φρονεῖν	*look down upon, despise, regard with contempt,* + gen.
1242 κατηγορεῖν	*accuse, charge, prosecute,* + gen. person; often with acc. also, as τοῦτό σου κατηγορῶ, 'this is what I'm charging you with' • Cf. n. κατηγορία²¹⁶, κατήγορος⁶²
1243 κινεῖν	*set in motion, stir up, disturb, meddle/ interfere with* (status quo); pass., *be set in motion, stir oneself, mobilise*
1244 κοσμεῖν	*arrange, adorn, embellish* • Cf. adj. κόσμιος⁵⁸¹, n. κόσμος⁶⁶
1245 κρατεῖν	+ gen., *be superior to, control, get possession of;* + acc., *master, overcome* • Cf. n. κράτος⁴³⁶
1246 ληρεῖν	*talk nonsense, rubbish*
1247 λοιδορεῖν	*abuse verbally,* + acc.; also middle, *hurl abuse at, inveigh against,* + dat. • Cf. n. λοιδορία²¹⁸
1248 λυπεῖν	*grieve, distress, irritate, annoy* • Cf. n. λύπη³⁰³
1249 λυσιτελεῖν	*profit,* usually impers., as λυσιτελεῖ μοι πείθεσθαι, 'it profits me to do/ I am better off doing as I am told'
1250 μαρτυρεῖν	*bear witness, give evidence, depose* • Cf. vb μαρτύρεσθαι¹¹¹⁶, n. μαρτυρία²²⁰, μάρτυς¹⁵²
1251 μισεῖν	*hate, detest*
1252 ναυμαχεῖν	*engage in a naval battle* • Cf. n. ναυμαχία²²³
1253 νοσεῖν	*be ill, diseased* (also metaphorical) • Cf. n. νόσος³⁴⁴
1254 νουθετεῖν	*admonish, lecture, counsel*
1255 οἰκεῖν	*live, reside;* + acc., *inhabit;* or, like δι-οικεῖν¹²¹⁴, *manage, govern;* ἡ οἰκουμένη *the Greek world, the inhabited world* • Cf. n. οἶκος⁸⁰
1256 οἰκοδομεῖν	*build a house, erect any structure* • Cf. n. οἰκοδόμημα⁴⁶²
1257 ὀκνεῖν	+ inf., *shrink from doing, hesitate, scruple to do* • Cf. n. ὄκνος⁸³

1258 ὀλιγωρεῖν   *treat lightly, be contemptuous of,* + gen.
- Cf. adj. ὀλίγωρος⁶⁵⁷, ὀλίγος⁵²⁰

1259 ὁμιλεῖν   *consort, associate, have intercourse* with (dat.)
- Cf. n. ὁμιλία²²⁵, ὅμιλος⁸⁵

1260 ὁμολογεῖν   *agree* (with: dat.; to: often fut. inf.), cf.
ὁμολογουμένως *by common consent; admit,
concede* that (ὅτι, or [acc. and] inf.)
- Cf. n. ὁμολογία²²⁶

1261 παρ-αινεῖν   *recommend, advise,* + dat. (and inf.)
- Cf. ἐπ-¹²²¹

1262 παρα-καλεῖν   *call to one's side, summon, invite; exhort,
encourage*

1263 πλεῖν   *sail, travel by sea*
- Cf. n. πλοῦς¹²⁸, πλοῖον⁴⁰⁹

1264 πλεονεκτεῖν   *gain/ have an advantage* (over: gen.); *seek to
take unfair advantage, be grasping*
- Cf. n. πλεονεξία²³⁵

1265 πλουτεῖν   *be rich, wealthy*
- Cf. adj. πλούσιος⁵⁹⁸, n. πλοῦτος⁹²

1266 ποιεῖν*   *make, do, cause* etc.
- Cf. vb προσ-ποιεῖσθαι¹³⁰⁹, n. ποίημα⁴⁶⁶,
ποίησις³⁵⁴, ποιητής¹⁷

1267 πολεμεῖν   *be at war, make war* (with: dat.)
- Cf. adj./ n. πολέμιος⁵⁹⁹, n. πόλεμος⁹³

1268 πολιορκεῖν   *besiege*
- Cf. n. πολιορκία²³⁶

1269 πονεῖν   *work hard, labour* (at: acc.), *be afflicted, hard
pressed,* (w. or without acc.) *suffer*
- Cf. n. πόνος⁹⁴

1270 προ-χωρεῖν   *go forward: prosper, succeed;* also impers., as
οὐ προυχώρει αὐτῷ, 'it was not going well for
him', 'he was not succeeding'

1271 πωλεῖν   *sell, offer for sale*

1272 ῥεῖν   *flow*

1273 σκοπεῖν   *look into, consider, examine*
- Cpd: ἐπι-¹²²⁷

1274 στρατηγεῖν   *hold the office of/be a general* (of a force: gen.)
- Cf. n. στρατηγός¹⁰⁴

1275 συγ-χωρεῖν   *give way, yield, assent* (to: dat.); *concede, give
up,* + acc., or *concede* that ..., acc. and inf.
(alternatively ὅτι/ ὡς)

1276 συκοφαντεῖν	be a συκοφάντης[22] (q.v.), + acc. prosecute one in that capacity
1277 σωφρονεῖν	be prudent, moderate etc., see s. adj. σώφρων[711] • Cf. also n. σωφροσύνη[327]
1278 ταλαιπωρεῖν	(or pass.) suffer, be subjected to misery, distress, hardship • Cf. adj. ταλαίπωρος[664]
1279 τελεῖν	fulfil, execute; pay, pay out • Cpd: δια-[1213] • Cf. n. τέλος[451]
1280 τηρεῖν	watch for/ over, guard, observe; keep watch
1281 ὑπηρετεῖν	serve, submit to, be an underling of, + dat. • Cf. n. ὑπηρέτης[24]
1282 φθονεῖν	be jealous of, resent, begrudge, + dat. • Cf. n. φθόνος[114]
1283 φιλεῖν	love, be fond of, like, also kiss; often + inf., be accustomed, tend to • Opp.: μισεῖν[1251] • Cf. n. φιλία[253], adj. φίλιος[616], φίλος[539]; vb ἀγαπᾶν[1143]
1284 φιλοσοφεῖν	love/ pursue knowledge, study philosophy • Cf. n. φιλόσοφος[115]
1285 φλυαρεῖν	talk nonsense, play the fool, often + acc., as πολλὰ φλυαρεῖν • Cf. n. φλυαρία[255]
1286 φρονεῖν*	think in a certain way • Cpd: κατα-[1241] • Cf. n. φρόνησις[364], adj. φρόνιμος[666]
1287 φρουρεῖν	keep guard, keep a look-out; + acc., guard, watch, garrison a place • Cf. n. φρουρά[256], φρουρός[119]
1288 χειροτονεῖν	elect (by show of hands), vote for • Cf. n. χείρ[384], vb τείνειν[1049]
1289 χωρεῖν	advance, come, go; + acc., contain, have room for • Cpd: ἀνα-[1191] προ-[1270] συγ-[1275]
1290 ψοφεῖν	make a noise • Cf. n. ψόφος[125]
1291 ὠθεῖν	thrust, shove, push hard, force; middle, force back, dislodge enemy

72

1292 ὠφελεῖν

benefit, help
• Cf. n. ὠφελία²⁶⁰, adj. ὠφέλιμος⁶⁶⁷

C.2 Infinitive in -εῖσθαι

1293 ἀπ-αρνεῖσθαι

deny that, μή + inf., as ἀπαρνεῖται μὴ ἀληθὲς εἶναι τοῦτο, 'he denies that this is true'

1294 ἀπο-λογεῖσθαι

speak in defence, defend oneself; + acc., *plead, allege* a point *in one's defence*
• Cf. n. ἀπολογία¹⁷⁸

1295 ἀρνεῖσθαι

deny, cf. s. ἀπ-αρνεῖσθαι¹²⁹³

1296 ἀφ-ικνεῖσθαι

arrive, come, often with εἰς + acc.

1297 δεῖσθαι

ask, require, + gen. person and inf.; + acc. and inf., *require that ... should ...*

1298 δια-νοεῖσθαι*

have in mind etc.
• Cf. προ-¹³⁰⁸; -εῖν: ἐν-¹²²⁰ ἐπι-¹²²⁵
• Cf. n. διάνοια¹⁸⁸

1299 δι-ηγεῖσθαι

set out in detail, relate, explain

1300 ἐν-θυμεῖσθαι

think about, reflect on, consider (+ gen.); + ὅτι, *reflect that ...*
• Cf. προ-¹³⁰⁷

1301 ἐξ-ηγεῖσθαι

prescribe, dictate; expound, explain, relate

1302 ἐπι-μελεῖσθαι/ -μέλεσθαι

take care of, be in charge of, devote attention to, cultivate, + gen.

1303 εὐλαβεῖσθαι

beware, take care; + acc., *beware of*

1304 ἡγεῖσθαι

lead, + dat.; *believe, hold, regard,* + acc. and inf.
• Cpd: δι-¹²⁹⁹ ἐξ-¹³⁰¹
• Cf. n. ἡγεμών¹⁴⁴

1305 μιμεῖσθαι

mimic, imitate, represent

1306 προ-αιρεῖσθαι

choose deliberately, prefer; + inf., *choose* to do as a matter of deliberate policy
• Cf. n. προαίρεσις³⁵⁷

1307 προ-θυμεῖσθαι

be enthusiastic, zealous, determined (commonly w. inf., sts w. acc., *be enthusiastically committed to* a course of action etc.)
• Cf. ἐν-¹³⁰⁰; and προθυμία²⁴⁰, πρόθυμος⁶⁶¹

1308 προ-νοεῖσθαι

+ acc., *take thought for, think ahead about, take care to provide;* + gen., *provide for, make provision for*
• Cf. δια-¹²⁹⁸, and n. πρόνοια²⁴¹

1309 προσ-ποιεῖσθαι

pretend, profess (to: inf.)

1310 τιμωρεῖσθαι	(sts active -εῖν) *avenge, punish; actively assist*
	• Cf. n. τιμωρία[251]
1311 ὑπ-ισχνεῖσθαι	*promise* (to do: fut. inf.)
	• Cf. n. ὑπόσχεσις[363]
1312 φοβεῖσθαι	*be afraid, be afraid of/ fear;* commonly with
	μή/ μὴ οὐ, 'that/ that not'
	• Cf. adj. φοβερός[617], n. φόβος[116]
1313 ὠνεῖσθαι	*buy, purchase*
	• Cf. s. πρίασθαι[1142]

D.1 Infinitive in -οῦν

1314 ἀξιοῦν*	*consider worthy, think right* etc.
	• Cf. adj. ἄξιος[555]
1315 ἀτιμοῦν	*dishonour,* esp. *disfranchise*
	• Cf. vb ἀτιμάζειν[893], n. ἀτιμία[183], adj.
	ἄτιμος[641]
1316 βεβαιοῦν	*make good, confirm*
	• Cf. adj. βέβαιος[645]
1317 βιοῦν	*live, pass one's life*
	• Cf. n. βίος[37]
1318 δηλοῦν	*make clear, show, reveal,* often with part. (cf. s.
	adj. δῆλος[496]), as δηλώσει οὐ κατηγορήσας,
	'he will make it clear that he did not make an
	accusation'
1319 δουλοῦν	*enslave* (usually middle, pass. *be enslaved*)
	• Cf. vb δουλεύειν[915]
1320 ἐλευθεροῦν	*set free, liberate*
	• Cf. n. ἐλευθερία[193], adj. ἐλεύθερος[569]
1321 ζηλοῦν	*emulate* someone, *strive to attain* something,
	aspire to; envy one (for: gen.)
1322 ζημιοῦν	*fine, penalise, punish*
	• Cf. n. ζημία[208]
1323 κυκλοῦν	*encircle, surround*
	• Cf. n. κύκλος[67]
1324 μισθοῦν	*hire out,* middle *hire*
	• Cf. n. μισθός[74]
1325 πληροῦν	*fill full* (of: gen.), *equip* a ship with crew etc.,
	man
	• Cf. adj. πλήρης[688]

D.2 Infinitive in -οῦσθαι

1326 ἐναντιοῦσθαι — *oppose*, + dat.
          • Cf. adj./ n. ἐναντίος[570]

E.1 Infinitive in -ναι
E.1/1 Present

1327 ἀνα-τιθέναι — *dedicate* (statue etc.); *refer, attribute*

1328 ἀν-οιγνύναι — *open*

1329 ἀπ-εῖναι — *be away, absent*
          • Opp.: παρ-εῖναι[1364]

1330 ἀπ-ιέναι — *go away, depart*

1331 ἀπο-δεικνύναι — *display, produce; establish, appoint; establish*
by argument, demonstrate; render x *so and so,*
represent x *as* or *make* x *seem so and so*

1332 ἀπο-διδόναι — *give back, render what is due;* middle, *sell*

1333 ἀπ-ολλύναι — *destroy, ruin, lose;* pass., *be done for, perish*
          • Opp.: σῴζειν[1046]
          • Cf. n. ὄλεθρος[84]

1334 ἀφ-ιέναι — *let go, release, dismiss, relinquish*
          • Cf. cpd προ-ίεσθαι[1386]

1335 δεικνύναι — *show, point out*
          • Cpd: ἀπο-[1331] ἐπι-[1347]

1336 δια-τιθέναι — *dispose, treat, manage,* often 'in a certain way'
(adv.), as κακῶς διατιθέναι τὸ πρᾶγμα, 'deal
with the business badly', make a mess of it

1337 διδόναι — *grant, give, offer;* + acc. and inf., *grant that one*
might ...
          • Cpd: ἀπο-[1332] ἐκ-[1340] ἐπι-[1348] μετα-[1358]
παρα-[1363] προ-[1367]

1338 εἶναι* — *be* etc.
          • Cpd: ἀπ-[1329] ἐν-[1343] ἐξ-[1344] μετ-[1360] παρ-[1364]
περι-[1366] συν-[1369]
          • Cf. n. οὐσία[228] (ἐξουσία[196], περιουσία[234],
συνουσία[249]), adv. ὄντως[817]

1339 εἰσ-ιέναι — *go in, enter,* often with εἰς

1340 ἐκ-διδόναι — *give up, surrender, give in marriage*

1341 ἐμ-πιμπλάναι — *fill full* (of: gen.)

1342 ἐμ-πιμπράναι — *burn, set fire to*

1343 ἐν-εῖναι — *be in;* as impers., + dat. and inf., *be possible* for
one to, *in one's power* to

1344 ἐξ-εῖναι
be possible, permitted, used impers., as ἔξεστί μοι δίκας λαμβάνειν, 'I am permitted to obtain satisfaction'
• Cf. n. ἐξουσία[196]

1345 ἐξ-ιέναι
go/ come out, march out

1346 ἐπ-αν-ιέναι
return

1347 ἐπι-δεικνύναι
(more commonly middle in this sense) display, exhibit; also set out, point out, demonstrate

1348 ἐπι-διδόναι
give freely, bestow; intrans., increase, improve, develop

1349 ἐπ-ιέναι
go against, attack, + dat.; in part., following, succeeding

1350 ἐπι-τιθέναι
inflict, impose upon, + acc. and dat.; middle, + dat., apply oneself to, or against, attack

1351 ἐφ-ιστάναι
set one over (dat.) to watch/ supervise; middle/ pass. be set over, put in charge of (dat.)
• Cf. n. ἐπιστάτης[4]

1352 ἡμί
v.s. φάναι[1371]

1353 ἰέναι
go, come; ἴθι (δή) + imper. 'come (then)'
• Cpd: ἀπ-[1330] εἰσ-[1339] ἐξ-[1345] ἐπαν-[1346] ἐπ-[1349] παρ-[1365] προσ-[1368]

1354 ἱστάναι*
set up etc.
• Cpd: ἐφ-[1351] καθ-[1355]; -ασθαι: ἀν-[1378] ἀφ-[1379] ὑφ-[1388]

1355 καθ-ιστάναι*
establish, appoint, put/ bring into a certain condition or situation etc.

1356 κατ-αγνύναι
break in pieces, break, wreck

1357 κατα-τιθέναι
set down, put down as a payment; middle, leave to one side, store up, deposit; lay aside, settle differences

1358 μετα-διδόναι
grant one (dat.) a share of (gen.), allow one to participate in

1359 μετα-τιθέναι
transpose, transform, alter

1360 μετ-εῖναι
Impers., + dat. and gen., μέτεστί μοι τούτων 'there is a share to me of this' = 'I have a share in, participate in this'

1361 ὀμνύναι
swear (ὅρκον ὀμνύναι, 'swear an oath'), often with fut. inf., to do; + acc., swear by, as ὄμνυμι τὸν Δία, 'I swear by Zeus'

1362 ὀνινάναι
profit, benefit; middle, + part., have/ derive benefit from -ing

76

1363 παρα-διδόναι	hand over
1364 παρ-εῖναι*	be present
	• Opp.: ἀπεῖναι¹³²⁹
1365 παρ-ιέναι	pass by, of time pass, τὰ παρεληλυθότα past events, the past; come forward to speak (in public)
1366 περι-εῖναι	surpass, + gen.; be left over, surplus
	• Cf. n. περιουσία²³⁴
1367 προ-διδόναι	betray
	• Cf. n. προδοσία²³⁹, προδότης¹⁹
1368 προσ-ιέναι	come/ go near, approach, + dat.
1369 συν-εῖναι	be with, associate with (dat.)
	• Cf. n. συνουσία²⁴⁹
1370 τιθέναι*	put, place etc.
	• Cpd: ἀνα-¹³²⁷ δια-¹³³⁶ ἐπι-¹³⁵⁰ κατα-¹³⁵⁷ μετα-¹³⁵⁹; -εσθαι: συν-¹³⁸⁷
1371 φάναι*	say
1372 χρή (χρῆναι)	Impers., it is necessary, right, (one) must, ought (commonly with acc. person and inf.)

E.1/2 Perfect

1373 δεδιέναι/ δεδοικέναι	fear, be afraid (of), often with acc. or μή
	• Cf. n. δέος⁴²³
1374 εἰδέναι*	know, be aware of
	• Cpd: συν-¹³⁷⁷
1375 εἰωθέναι	be accustomed, in the habit of (+ inf.)
1376 ἐοικέναι*	resemble, + dat.; seem, seem likely
	• Cf. adv. εἰκότως⁷⁶⁴
1377 συν-ειδέναι	be aware, realise, + part. or dat. and part., as σύνοιδα οὐδὲν ἐπιστάμενος or σύνοιδα ἐμαυτῷ οὐδὲν ἐπισταμένῳ, 'I am conscious of the fact that I know nothing'

E.2 Infinitive in -σθαι

1378 ἀν-ίστασθαι	stand up, get to one's feet
1379 ἀφ-ίστασθαι	distance/ dissociate oneself, withdraw, revolt from (gen.)
1380 διά-κεισθαι	be disposed, have an attitude, be in a frame of mind/ condition, with adv., ἀθλίως διέκειντο, 'they were in a sorry mess'

1381 δύνασθαι	*be able, capable,* + inf.; *be influential,* as μέγα δυνάμεθα παρὰ τῷ τυράννῳ, 'we have great influence with the tyrant'; *mean, signify*
	• Cf. n. δύναμις[350], adj. δυνατός[497]
1382 ἐπίστασθαι	*understand, have (expert, specialist) knowledge of; know how to* (inf.)
	• Cf. n. ἐπιστήμη[292], adj. ἐπιστήμων[709]
1383 καθ-ῆσθαι	*be seated, sit,* sts *sit doing nothing, idly*
1384 κεῖσθαι	*have been put: have lain (down), lie (down), lie buried;* of a law, *have been put = be instituted/ framed* or *established*
	• Cpd: διά-[1380]
1385 μεμνῆσθαι [perf.]	Cf. s. μιμνήσκεσθαι[1120]
1386 προ-ίεσθαι (προ-ίημι)	*give up, abandon, throw away, squander*
	• Cf. cpd ἀφ-ιέναι[1334]
1387 συν-τίθεσθαι	*make an agreement* (dat., with one); + acc., *agree on* (with: dat.); + inf. (often fut.) *agree to do*
	• Cf. n. συνθῆκαι[325], αἱ
1388 ὑφ-ίστασθαι	*promise, undertake,* w. or without (fut.) inf.; + acc., *submit to, consent to, shoulder*

V. OTHER WORDS

Assembled here are the most important conjunctions, (cor)relatives, particles and pronouns

1389 ἀλλά   *but, but rather, on the contrary;* (indicating acquiescence) *very well,* (+ imp.) *come now*

1390 ἀλλήλους -ας -α   [no nominative!] *each other, one another*
     • Cf. next

1391 ἄλλος* -η -ο   *other, remaining, rest of*
     • Cf. ἄλλη[738], ἄλλως[742]; ἀλλήλους[1390], ἀλλοῖος[551]; ἀλλότριος[552]; ἄλλοθεν[739], ἄλλοθι[740], ἄλλοσε[741]

1392 ἀμφότεροι -αι -α   *both (parties, sides)*
     • Cf. adv. ἀμφοτέρωθεν[744]

— ἄν   = ἐάν[1407], q.v.

1393 ἄν*   Postp. modal particle

1394 ἄπας ἄπασα ἄπαν   = πᾶς[1469]

1395 ἆρα   Particle introducing a question, commonly ἆρ' οὐ in expectation of an affirmative reply

1396 ἄρα   Postp. particle, *then* (inferentially), *all along, after all, when all is said and done;* εἰ ἄρα *if after all, if by any chance, if it turns out that ...*

1397 ἅτε   + part., *seeing that, inasmuch as*
     • Cf. s. οἷος[1444]

1398 αὐτός* -ή -ό   (Neut. also ταὐτόν = τὸ αὐτόν) *him* etc./ *-self/ same*
     • Cf. adj. αὐτάρκης[678], αὐτόματος[492], αὐτόνομος[643]; n. αὐτόμολος[35]; adv. αὐτόθεν[756], αὐτόθι[757], αὐτοῦ[758]

1399 γάρ   Postp. particle, *for* (sts *for otherwise*), *because* (often '<yes> because', '<no> because'), *since;* καὶ γάρ 'since in point of fact'; cf. s. δή[1403]

1400 γε   Postp. particle, emphatic or limitative, *certainly, indeed, at least, at any rate;* also *yes*

1401 γοῦν   Postp. particle, *at any rate, anyhow; certainly, yes certainly*

1402 δέ	Postp. particle, *and, then, but, whereas;* cf. s. μέν[1433]
1403 δή*	Postp. particle, *indeed, certainly* etc.
1404 δήπου	Postp. particle, *used diffidently or confidently, presumably, doubtless, surely*
1405 δῆτα	Postp. particle, *indeed,* w. interrogatives *then*
1406 διό	(i.e. δι' [760] ὅ[1454]) *for this reason, hence*
1407 ἐάν	= εἰ[1410] + ἄν[1393], *if,* w. subjv. in prospective or general condition (alternative forms ἄν, ἤν)
1408 ἑαυτόν -ήν -ό	(also αὐτόν etc.) *himself* etc. (reflexive); in gen., *his* etc. *own* • Cf. ἐμαυτόν[1418], σ(ε)αυτόν[1486]
1409 ἐγώ	(plur. ἡμεῖς) *I*
1410 εἰ	*if, supposing, whether,* εἰ δὲ μή *otherwise;* sts of an admitted fact, *since, because* • Cf. s. ἐάν[1407], and εἴπερ[1412]; εἴτε[1414]
1411 εἶεν	(used in argument) *so far so good, well now, right then*
1412 εἴπερ	*if in fact, if really/ genuinely, if indeed;* = ἐπείπερ, *since in fact, given that* (cf. εἰ[1410])
1413 εἷς μία ἕν	*one, a single, one and the same* • Cf. οὐδείς[1462]
1414 εἴτε	Duplicated, *whether/ either ... or*
1415 ἕκαστος -η -ον	*each,* regularly with article, as ἑκάστη ἡ ἡμέρα, 'every single day'; plur. *each party, side* etc. • Cf. adv. ἑκάστοτε[769], and next
1416 ἑκάτερος -α -ον	*each of two;* plur. *either side* etc.
1417 ἐκεῖνος -η -ο	*that,* sts *the famous, the former;* also serves as emphatic third person pronoun, *'he'* etc.; ἐκείνη *in that quarter/ in that fashion* • Cf. adv. ἐκεῖ[770] ἐκεῖθεν[771] ἐκεῖσε[772]
1418 ἐμαυτόν -ήν	*myself;* in gen., *my own* • Cf. ἑαυτόν[1408], σ(ε)αυτόν[1486]
1419 ἔνιοι -αι -α	*some* • Cf. adv. ἐνίοτε[781]
1420 ἐπεί/	*when, since, because* (note also ἐπειδάν = ἐπεί
1421 ἐπειδή	+ ἄν)
1422 ἕτερος -α -ον	*other of two;* w. article, *the other* or *one of two*
1423 ἕως	*while, as long as; until*
1424 ἤ	*or,* ἤ ... ἤ *either ... or; than*

1425 ἦ	Particle, *indeed, really, surely,* in questions *can it indeed/ in fact be the case that ...?* etc.
1426 ᾗ	Adv., *at/ to which point; as*
— ἥν	= ἐάν[1407], q.v.
1427 ἡνίκα	*at the time when, when*
1428 ἵνα	*in order that*
1429 καί*	*and, even* etc., see Supp.
1430 καίπερ	+ part., *although*
1431 καίτοι	*and yet, yet, but;* sts *and indeed*
1432 μά*	Asseverative particle
1433 μέν	Postp. particle, regularly found in first member of antithesis (expressed or implied); commonly answered by δέ[1402]
1434 μέντοι*	Postp. particle
1435 μέχρι	Conj., *until* or *as long as* (also μέχρι οὗ); + gen., *as far as, up to* (a place or point in time)
1436 μήν*	Postp. particle
1437 μῶν	*surely ... not?*
1438 ναί	*yes*
1439 νή	Asseverative particle, + accus., as νὴ (τὸν) Δία, literally 'yes by Zeus': cf. under μά[1432]
1440 ὁ* ἡ τό	Definite article, *the,* and also a pronoun
1441 ὅδε ἥδε τόδε	*this* (often used with ref. to someone or something which is here before one, here right now), *the following;* τῇδε adverbially *in this way, in the following way*
1442 ὅθεν	*from which place, on what ground/ for what reason* (cf. under πόθεν[1473]/ ποθεν[1474])
1443 οἷ	*to what place, where* • Cf. ὅποι[1447]
1444 οἷος* -α -ον	*the kind of person who/ thing which* etc. • Cf. ὁποῖος[1448]
1445 ὅμως	*nonetheless, still, despite that;* commonly ὅμως δέ, ἀλλ᾽ ὅμως; ὅμως μέντοι[1434] 'nevertheless, for all that'
1446 ὅπη	*by which way* or *in what way, as* • Cf. πῇ[1470]
1447 ὅποι	[direct form ποῖ] *to which/ what place* • Cf. οἷ[1443]
1448 ὁποῖος -α -ον	In indirect questions, *what sort, kind of ...* • Cf. ποῖος[1477], and οἷος[1444]

81

¹⁴⁴⁹ ὁπόσος -η -ον	In indirect questions, *how much, how many* etc.; or as relative, *as much/ many as, all that ...* etc. (cf. ὅσος¹⁴⁵⁵) • Cf. πόσος¹⁴⁷⁸
¹⁴⁵⁰ ὁπόταν/ ὁπότε	*when(ever)*, + subjv. (form ὁπόταν) or optat.; sts causal, + indic., *seeing that*, cf. ὅτε¹⁴⁵⁸ • Cf. πότε¹⁴⁷⁹
¹⁴⁵¹ ὁπότερος -α -ον	*which of two; either of two* • Cf. πότερος¹⁴⁸¹
¹⁴⁵² ὅπου	[direct form ποῦ¹⁴⁸²] *in which/ what place, where, in circumstances in which* • Cf. οὗ¹⁴⁵⁹
¹⁴⁵³ ὅπως*	[direct form πῶς¹⁴⁸⁴] *in what way, how*
¹⁴⁵⁴ ὅς* ἥ ὅ	*who, which, that* • Cf. ᾗ¹⁴²⁶ adv.
¹⁴⁵⁵ ὅσος* -η -ον	*as much as* etc. • Cf. ὁπόσος¹⁴⁴⁹
¹⁴⁵⁶ ὅστις* ἥτις ὅτι	*whoever* etc.
¹⁴⁵⁷ ὁστισοῦν neut. ὁτιοῦν	*anybody/ anything whatsoever*, as τρόπῳ ἢ μηχανῇ ἡτινιοῦν, 'by any manner or means whatever'
¹⁴⁵⁸ ὅταν/ ὅτε	+ indic., *when, at the time when, now that* (ἔσθ' ὅτε *sometimes*); + subjv. (form ὅταν) or optat., *when(ever)*; sts causal, + indic., *seeing that*, cf. ὁπότε¹⁴⁵⁰
¹⁴⁵⁹ οὗ	= ὅπου¹⁴⁵²
¹⁴⁶⁰ οὗ	gen. (also enclitic οὑ), acc. ἕ (ἑ), dat. οἷ (οἱ): indirect reflexive, *him(self), her(self), it(self)*, in plur. σφᾶς etc. (this also with forms of αὐτός¹³⁹⁸, as σφᾶς αὐτούς)
¹⁴⁶¹ οὐδέ	*and/ but ... not, nor, (and) not even, (and) not ... either*
¹⁴⁶² οὐδείς οὐδεμία οὐδέν	*no one, no*, neut. *nothing , no* (or adverbial, *in no way, not at all*); οὐδὲν λέγειν opp. λέγειν τι, cf s. τις¹⁴⁹¹ • Cf. εἷς¹⁴¹³
¹⁴⁶³ οὐδέτερος -α -ον	*neither of the two*
¹⁴⁶⁴ οὐκοῦν	*therefore, accordingly, well then, very well*
¹⁴⁶⁵ οὔκουν	*not ... therefore/ then*

1466 οὖν

Postp. particle, *so, therefore, accordingly;*
δ' οὖν *at any rate, anyhow, be that as it may;*
μὲν οὖν often *no, rather, on the contrary*

1467 οὔτε

Duplicated, *neither ... nor*

1468 οὗτος* αὕτη τοῦτο

this, that
• Cf. οὕτω(ς)826

1469 πᾶς πᾶσα πᾶν

all, every, every kind of, any; + article, *the whole*
• Cf. ἅπας1394, σύμπας1488; and adv. πάντως834 etc., adj. παντοδαπός523, παντοῖος595

1470 πῇ

in what way, how (in direct or indirect question)
• Cf. ὅπῃ1446

1471 πῃ

in some/ any way (freq. accompanying another adv., as πῃ ἄλλη738 'in some other way'), *somehow*

1472 πλήν

except (also + gen.)

1473 πόθεν

where ... from? on what basis? for what reason? on what grounds?

1474 ποθεν

Postp., *from some place, from somewhere, on some basis*

1475 ποῖ

where ... to? in what direction?
• Cf. ὅποι1447

1476 ποι

Postp., *(to) somewhere, in some direction*

1477 ποῖος* -α -ον

what sort of?
• Cf. ὁποῖος1448

1478 πόσος -η -ον

how much/ great/ many?
• Cf. ὁπόσος1449

1479 πότε

when?
• Cf. ὁπότε1450

1480 ποτε*

Postp., *once* etc.
• Cf. οὐδέποτε823

1481 πότερος* -α -ον

which of the two?
• Cf. ὁπότερος1451

1482 ποῦ

where?
• Cf. ὅπου1452

1483 που

Postp., *somewhere — I suppose, one imagines, presumably, surely*

1484 πῶς

how?
• Cf. ὅπως1453

1485 πως

Postp., *somehow, in some way or other,* εἴ πως 'if somehow', 'in the hope of finding some way

83

of'; ἄλλως[742] πως 'in some other way', ὧδέ[864] πως 'in some such way as this'

1486 σ(ε)αυτόν -ήν   *yourself,* in gen. *your own*
  • Cf. ἑαυτόν[1408], ἐμαυτόν[1418]

1487 σύ   *you* (plur. ὑμεῖς)

1488 σύμπας -πασα -παν   *all together, all told;* in sing. + article, *the whole* x *together,* x *taken as a whole*
  • Cf. ἅπας[1394], πᾶς[1469]

— σφεῖς   See οὗ[1460]

1489 τε   Postp. particle, τε ... καί *both ... and;* smts τε alone = *and, and so, thus*

1490 τίς neut. τί   *who? what? which?* In neut. also *why? in what respect? to what extent? by what means?* τίς οὐ ...; *i.e. 'surely everybody ...'*

1491 τις* neut. τι   Postp., *some(one), some(thing)* etc.
  • Cf. ὅστις[1456]

1492 τοι   Postp. particle, *in truth, let me tell you, I can assure you, mark my words*

1493 τοίνυν   Postp. particle, *so then, accordingly, well now; furthermore* (cf. s. ἔτι[790])

1494 τοιόσδε -άδε -όνδε   *such as this/ as follows*
  • Cf. next

1495 τοιοῦτος -αύτη -οῦτο(ν)   *such, of this/ that kind/ nature*

1496 τοσοῦτος -αύτη -οῦτο(ν)   *so much, so great, so large* etc., *so small;* plur., *so many, so numerous, so few*

1497 ὦ   Commonly prefaces vocative; in exclamations, as ὦ πρὸς τῶν θεῶν, 'in heaven's name', 'I ask you!'

1498 ὡς*   has various senses: see Supp.

1499 ὥσπερ   *just as, as, as if*

1500 ὥστε   *so that, so as, that* (expressing result); often in argument/ narrative *consequently, hence*

SUPPLEMENT

ἀγαθός[489]
- *good (efficient, talented, successful)* in various respects (e.g. ἀγαθὸς ποιητής, 'a good, accomplished poet', ἀγαθὸς ἦν τὰ πολιτικά, 'he was good in respect of the city's affairs', i.e. 'he was an able statesman'), particularly *good at fighting, brave*
- Often *beneficial* ~ in neut. *a benefit, service, blessing;* τὰ ἀγαθά also *property, wealth, assets*
- κρείττων = *superior*, usually in power, *stronger,* + gen. *superior to, in control of;* in neut. *better, more advantageous, advisable* [so ἄμεινον often] to ...)
- ὦ ἄριστε freq. in address *my excellent friend* sim., and so ὦ βέλτιστε, ὠγαθέ

ἄγειν[867]
- *lead, conduct, bring, take,* when what is taken etc. is living (ctr. φέρειν[1069]: ἄγειν καὶ φέρειν is a set phrase = 'ravage, plunder')
- *celebrate, observe* festival (ἑορτήν) etc., εἰρήνην ἄγειν 'be at, observe, maintain peace'
- Middle freq. *bring oneself* a wife into the household

ἀγωνίζεσθαι[1078]
- *compete, contend, struggle* (in a contest: acc.), often + περί and gen., = for, over
- *be on trial, contest a case* (ἀγῶνα[133], δίκην[287], γραφήν[282]) in court

ἀδικεῖν[1182]
- *be dishonest, commit a crime* (often + acc., as πόλλ' ἠδίκηκε, 'he has committed a number of crimes'; cf. ἀδικίαν or ἀδίκημα ἀδικεῖν, 'inflict a wrong', in pass. -ιαν/ -ημα ἀδικεῖσθαι 'have a wrong inflicted on one'), or *be guilty*
- With personal object, *injure, wrong, commit a crime against,* πόλλ' ἠδίκηκε τὴν πόλιν '... against the state'

ἀεί[737]
- + part., *at any given time/ point, in any given case,* e.g. δεῖ τὸν ἀεὶ ληφθέντα δίκην διδόναι, 'it is necessary that the individual caught each time (~ each and every offender once apprehended) should be punished'

αἱρεῖν[1185] ~ αἱρεῖσθαι
* *capture, seize, take*, often *convict* in a court of law
* Middle *choose, elect* (in aor., and also perf., pass. *be chosen, be elected)*; + inf.
(cf. προ-αιρεῖσθαι[1081]) *choose, prefer* to

αἰσθάνεσθαι[1079]
* *perceive, notice, realise*, with ὅτι or ὡς, but more commonly with gen. or gen.
(sts acc.) + part. (e.g. αἰσθάνεταί σου φεύγοντος, 'he notices that you are trying
to get away')
* Also with nominative part., as ᾔσθετο κάμνων, 'he realised that he was ill'

αἴτιος[549]
* *responsible, to blame* (for something: gen., often with a complementary personal
dat., lit. 'for ...', as αἴτιον σφίσιν ἐνόμιζον πάντων ὧν ἔπασχον, 'they considered
him to blame for them(selves) for all (the things) which they were suffering', i.e.
'they held him responsible for all they were undergoing')
* N.B. τὸ αἴτιον *cause*

ἀκούειν[872]
* *hear, listen to,* + acc. of thing heard; commonly + personal gen. (and part.), as
ἀκούει σου διαλεγομένου, 'he can hear you conversing'
* + adv., *be spoken of,* as κακῶς ἀκούει ὑπὸ τοῦ δήμου [cf. under λέγειν in
Supplement]; alternatively, with nominative, κόλακες[148] ἀκούουσιν

ἄκρος[550]
* *(relating to) the top, surface, edge, extremity of,* e.g. ἐπ᾽ ἄκρῳ τῷ σώματι, 'on
the body's surface', ἄκραι χεῖρες καὶ πόδες, 'fingers and toes'
* *supreme, pre-eminent*, as ἄκρος ἰατρός[58]
* τὸ ἄκρον *extremity,* (literal or metaphorical) *summit, peak, pinnacle*

ἄκων[712]
* *unwilling, involuntary,* hence *unwillingly, involuntarily,* English preferring to use
an adverb or adverbial phrase, as ἄκουσα ἐξέβαλεν αὐτόν, 'she ejected him
reluctantly/ with reluctance'
* *Not* used predicatively, as in 'I am unwilling'

ἄλλος[1391]
* *other, remaining, rest of:* note οἱ ἄλλοι 'the rest', 'everybody else', τἆλλα [= τὰ
ἄλλα] πάντα 'everything else', ὁ ἄλλος στρατός 'the remainder of the force' —
Also common in the sense *as well, besides,* as ἠμύνατο τοὺς ὁπλίτας καὶ τοὺς

ἄλλους ἱππέας, 'he repulsed the hoplites and the others viz. the cavalry', i.e. '...
and the cavalry into the bargain'
• ἄλλο ἤ 'other than, quite unlike'; ἄλλο τι ἤ or just ἄλλο τι, '<is it> something
else (or)', is used to preface questions confidently expecting an affirmative reply

ἄλλως[742]
• *otherwise, differently* (μὴ ἄλλως ποίει 'don't act otherwise', i.e. 'do as I say',
'don't say no')
• Also *to no purpose, ineffectually*
• ἄλλως τε καί ... *especially, in particular*

ἅμα[743]
• *at the same time, also, in addition* (ἅμα μέν ... ἅμα δέ 'partly ... partly')
• + dat., *at the same time as, simultaneously with* (e.g. ἅμ᾽ ἕῳ γιγνομένῃ 'as day
began to dawn'); of accompaniment, *together with*

ἄν[1393]
• Postp. modal particle, used to express *would, could, should, may, might* ...; found
in various dependent clauses, as indefinite clauses introduced by ὅταν[1458] = ὅτε +
ἄν, + subjv.
• ἄν + imperfect can express *repeated* action, our 'he would say' = 'was in the
habit of saying'

ἄνθρωπος[30]
• *human being, man* (plur. *mankind*, οὐδεὶς ἀνθρώπων 'nobody in the world') as
opposed to god/ animal
• Often derogatory, *person, character* etc., ἄνθρωπος or ὁ ἄνθρωπος *the fellow*; ἡ
female

ἄξιος[555]
• *worthy, deserving* (of: gen.)
• Also + inf., ταῦτ᾽ οὐκ ἄξια λέγειν, 'these points are not worth mentioning', or
acc. and inf., ἄξιον ὑμᾶς ὀργὴν ἔχειν, '<it's> proper that you should feel anger'
• Note too ἡ ἀξία *value, price, worth*

ἀξιοῦν[1314]
• *consider worthy, think right*, + acc. and gen., as ἀξιῶ σε ἐπαίνου, 'I consider
you deserving of commendation'; + inf., as ἀξιοῦμεν λέγειν, 'we think it right
that we should speak'; + acc. and inf., ἀξιοῖ σε ζημιοῦσθαι, 'he thinks it
appropriate/ insists that you should be penalised'

ἄρχειν[892]
* *hold office, rule* (over: gen.)
* *begin, take the initiative* (in: gen.), or *begin* from/ with a point (gen. or ἀπό + gen.) — In middle, *begin,* commonly + part., ἄρχεται κελεύων 'he begins to give orders'

ἀρχή[274]
* *beginning,* commonly *starting-point, first principle/ initial assumption;* τὴν ἀρχήν *at all* is freq. in neg. sentences
* Also common in the sense *office, magistracy,* plur. *office-holders, magistrates, the authorities; rule, empire — government, regime*

αὐτός[1398]
* As postp., unemphatic 3rd person pronoun, *him her it them,* e.g. ἤκουσα αὐτῆς ᾀδούσης, 'I heard her singing'. Neut. plur. αὐτά often 'the topic in hand', 'the point under consideration'
* To express *-self,* as αὐτὴ ταῦτ' ἐποίουν, 'I was in the process of doing this myself/ personally/ on my own/ unaided', with article δεῖ τιμᾶν αὐτὴν τὴν [contrast word-order in next example] ἀλήθειαν, 'truth itself/ the actual truth ought to be respected'
* Article + αὐτός = *the same,* as εἰσέδραμεν εἰς τὴν αὐτὴν οἰκίαν, 'he ran into the same house'; 'same as': the dat. is used, ὁ αὐτὸς νόμος τῷδε, 'the same regulation as this present one', alternatively καί[1429]

βούλεσθαι[1093]
* *be willing, wish, want,* + inf.; commonly in dat. part. + εἶναι, λέξω ὅτι ἂν πρῶτον ἀκούειν βουλομένοις ὑμῖν ᾖ, 'I'll relate whatever you want to hear first'; ὁ βουλόμενος 'anyone who/ whoever wishes/ is willing'
* βούλει followed up with deliberative subjv., βούλει δεώμεθ' αὐτοῦ τοῦ μάρτυρος ταῦτ' ἐπιδεῖξαι; 'are we to ask the witness personally to demonstrate this?'

γίγνεσθαι[1095]
* *come into being, become, (prove to) be* (sts *find oneself, arrive* at a point; + ἐν, *be engaged* in an activity), *amount to, be done, happen, take place* (often in part., τὰ γενόμενα, τὰ γεγενημένα)
* Also serves as pass. of ποιεῖσθαι, as λόγους ποιοῦνται 'they are making speeches' ~ λόγοι γίγνονται 'speeches are being made'

γιγνώσκειν⁹⁰⁰

• *get to know, perceive, recognise, realise* (commonly + part., ἔγνωσαν ἐξηπατημένοι, 'they realised that they had been deceived'; or + ὅτι, or relative words such as οἷος)

• *judge, determine* (sts + inf.), *reach a verdict*

δεῖν¹²¹⁰ (B)

• *be necessary*, as impers., + inf. or acc. and inf., as τί δεῖ ποιεῖν; 'what's to be done?', ἔδει σ' ἀπολογήσασθαι, 'you ought to have defended yourself', 'you had to defend yourself'; also τὰ δέοντα, 'the necessary/ obligatory things', 'one's duty'

• *there is need of*, with gen. and dat., as δεῖ μοι τούτων, 'I need this'. Also personally, as τοσούτου δέω ταῦθ' ὁμολογεῖν, ὥστε ..., i.e. 'so far am I from admitting this that ...' (cf. also s. adj. ὀλίγος⁵²⁰)

δεινός⁴⁹⁵

• *fearful, formidable, terrible, scandalous, appalling*, etc., also freq. *dangerous, serious* (τὸ δεινόν *danger, threat*)

• *clever, ingenious*, often + inf., λέγειν πάντων δεινότατος 'the cleverest of all speakers'

δή¹⁴⁰³

• Postp. particle, *indeed, certainly*, often ironic or sarcastic (+ imp. *come now, then, just, please*, in admonition *be warned*), commonly emphasising previous word, as πάντες δή 'absolutely everyone' (in English the force would often be conveyed by tone of voice, facial expression, gesture)

• γὰρ δή 'because indeed/ beyond a doubt'

• μὲν δή commonly closes a topic, 'well then, right then'

• καὶ δὴ καί passing from generalities to the subject of immediate interest, 'and in particular, specifically'

δῆλος⁴⁹⁶

• Note adverbial δῆλα δή or δηλαδή, 'quite obviously', and the elliptical δῆλον ὅτι or δηλονότι, 'clearly', '— that's clear —'

• Often used personally, δῆλος εἶ ἀγανακτῶν, 'it is clear that you are irritated', 'you are plainly annoyed'

διανοεῖσθαι¹²⁹⁸

• *have in mind* to do, *intend, plan*, + inf. (often fut.)

• *think, suppose* that, + acc. and inf.

• + adv., *be disposed* in a certain way

διδάσκειν911

• *teach,* often with double acc. (one a thing); middle, *have/ get* someone *taught*
• Also commonly *explain,* with personal acc. *instruct* one, *explain to* one, *put* one *in the picture*

δίκαιος567

• Very often used personally, + inf., δίκαιος εἶ ἀγαθόν τι ποιῆσαι τὴν γυναῖκα, 'it's right that you should do/ you're justified in doing the woman a good turn'

δίκη287

• *lawsuit:* esp. private action, as opposed to γραφή282, q.v.
• *legal satisfaction:* note (sing. or plur.) δίκας λαμβάνειν 'obtain satisfaction', 'win redress' (from: παρά + gen.), δίκην διδόναι, 'give satisfaction', 'be chastised' (+ gen., e.g. τῶν ἠδικημένων, 'for crimes committed')

δοκεῖν1215

• *think, fancy* that, + (acc. and) inf.
• *be thought, have a reputation, seem,* as δοκεῖ αἴτιος εἶναι τῆς συμφορᾶς, 'he is considered to be responsible for the setback', οὐκ ἄν μοι δοκεῖς ἁμαρτάνειν, 'not would to me you seem to make a mistake', i.e. 'I don't think you would ...'
• Also *seem good, appropriate,* impers., as ἔδοξε τῷ δήμῳ τὰς ναῦς ἀποστέλλειν, 'the assembly decided to dispatch the fleet'

εἰδέναι1374

• *know, be aware of,* often with part. or acc. and part., as οἶδα πολλὰ χρήματ' ἀναλίσκων, 'I know that I'm spending a lot of money', ἴσμεν ὑμᾶς ἐθέλοντας ἀναβαίνειν, 'we are aware that you are willing to embark'
• οἶδ' ὅτι parenthetically, 'I'm sure/ convinced', cf. δηλονότι (δῆλος496 Supplement)

εἶναι1338

• *be, be the case* (ἔστι ταῦτα 'that's true'), *exist*
• ἔστι often = ἔξεστι, *it's possible*
• τῷ ὄντι *in reality, really*
• τὰ ὄντα *one's property*
• + dat. person, 'there is to me' = 'I have, own'

ἐναντίος570

• + dat.: τἀναντία ὑμῖν αὐτοῖς λέγετε, 'you are contradicting yourselves'
• τοὐναντίον adverbially = *on the contrary*

- As noun, *opponent, enemy*
- As prep. + gen., *in the presence of, in front of*

ἐοικέναι[1376]

- *seem, seem likely:* often ὡς ἔοικε, 'as it seems, so it appears'
- Neut. part. εἰκός: *reasonable, probable, likely* that one *would* etc., as εἰκὸς ἦν σ' ἀπεῖναι, 'it was reasonable to expect that you would be away'; τὸ εἰκός *likelihood, probability*
- Also ὡς εἰκός, ὡς τὸ εἰκός 'naturally enough', 'in all probability', similarly κατὰ [opposite παρὰ] τὸ εἰκός

ἐπί[788]

- Very elastic: main uses recorded here:
- + acc., *on to, up to, against, over, for the space of, for the purpose of, to get, to fetch*
- + gen., *upon, in the direction of, in the time of, on the occasion of*
- + dat., *on, against, with a view to, in the case of, in the power of, on condition of* (ἐφ᾽ ᾧ/ ᾧτε + [acc. and] inf. or fut. indic. 'on condition that ...'), *in addition to*

ἐπιτήδειος[571]

- Applied to people, *of service, friendly;* often as noun, *close friend, intimate,* φίλος καὶ ἐπιτήδειος 'a close personal friend'
- τὰ ἐπιτήδεια *necessaries, supplies, provisions*

ἔργον[396]

- *piece of work* esp. *work of art; deed, action* (sts *military engagement), achievement; function; fact, reality,* commonly opp. to λόγος[71] what is said or claimed (type λόγῳ μέν/ ἔργῳ δέ and similar)

ἐρωτᾶν[1153]

- *ask* one a question, often with:
impers. object (γελοῖον ἐρωτᾷς 'A ridiculous question!')
double acc. ('ask one something')
acc. and εἰ, 'whether'

ἔτι[790]

- *still* (note ἔτι καὶ νῦν, *even now, to this very day), after this, hereafter* (with Comp. *still, yet more ...*)
- ἔτι δέ or ἔτι τοίνυν[1493] '(and) what is more'

ἔχειν[943]
• *have, possess, hold*
• + inf., *be able;* with dependent clause, *know*, as οὐκ ἔχω τί λέγω, 'I don't know what (I am) to say'
• + adv., *be;* εὖ ἔχειν + gen. 'be well off for', 'have plenty of'
• Middle + gen. *cling to, cleave to; border on; pertain to*

ἡδύς[700]
• *sweet, pleasant, pleasurable, enjoyable*
• Adv. ἡδέως literally *with pleasure* is commonly used in expressions like ἡδέως ἂν ἡγοίμην, 'I'd like to lead the way', ἥδιον ἂν ἐξέβαλον αὐτόν, 'I'd rather have thrown him out'

ἱστάναι[1354]
• *set up, make to stand/ bring to a standstill, station, establish*
• Intrans., *be stationed* or *stationary, take one's stand, stand*

καθ-ιστάναι[1355]
• *establish, appoint, put/ bring* into a certain condition or situation, as τοὺς πολεμίους εἰς φυγὴν κατέστησαν, 'they put the enemy to flight', εἰς ἀγῶνα κατέστη, 'he was brought to trial'
• Intrans. in perf., *have come into a certain (irreversible) state, be in a certain predicament; be established/ current, prevail*, τὰ καθεστηκότα *established institutions, the established order*

καί[1429]
• *and*, καὶ ... καί *both ... and;* cf. under τε
• *actually, in fact, even, also* (in disjunctions εἴτε or ἢ καί, 'or alternatively, if you like')
• = *as, to*, with words expressing sameness/ similarity, notably ὁ αὐτός[1398], ὅμοιος[592]

κακός[506]
• *bad*, especially *cowardly, wicked*, or *inflicting evil, pernicious, ruinous*
• κακόν neut. *a bad thing, misfortune, trouble, malady* etc.
• Comp. κακίων, ἥττων (*inferior*), χείρων (*inferior*, often *worthless*), Sup. κάκιστος, χείριστος (*worst, lowest* socially)
• Opp.: ἀγαθός

καλός[507]

• *commendable, admirable, good* in some respect (cf. καλῶς πράττειν = εὖ πράττειν, 'fare well'); *handsome, beautiful*, alternatively *creditable, honourable* (τὸ καλόν often contrasted with τὸ αἰσχρόν)
• Sts ironic, *fine*

κατά[796]

• + acc., (locally) *down, throughout, on, by, opposite, over against; in the course of, during; for the purpose of, in quest of; in accordance with, in the style of, in relation to* (τὸ κατ᾽ ἐμέ, 'as far as I am concerned'); (distributively) *by* (so many) *at a time, in* (distinct units)
• + gen., *down from/ over/ into; concerning, in relation to;* (swear) *by, over; against, to the detriment of*

λέγειν[981]

• *speak, tell, say, mean* (as πῶς λέγεις; 'how do you mean?', λέγων τὴν πόλιν 'meaning the city')
• + ὅτι, ὡς or acc. and inf., *say* that
• With acc. person, εὖ λέγειν/ κακῶς λέγειν 'speak well/ badly' of one [cf. under ἀκούειν in Supplement]
• Also + inf., *tell* one to do

λόγος[71]

• *word* (often λόγῳ *in theory* opp. ἔργῳ[396]), *speech, expression, account, argument, debate* etc.
• *reason, reasoning, ground, principle*
• *account, consideration,* as λόγον ποιεῖσθαι + gen. 'attach weight to'

μά[1432]

• + acc., ναὶ[1438] μὰ τὸν Δία, 'yes by Zeus', οὐ μὰ τὸν Δία 'no by Zeus'; also used in a negative utterance, as μὰ Δί᾽ οὐκ ἔχω σοι λέγειν, 'I'm just not able to tell you' Cf. under νή[1439]

μέγας[715]

• *big, spacious, tall, great, important, serious, grave, severe, strong* etc.
• Adv. μάλα, *very, very much,* in replies *very much so, quite* — Comp. μᾶλλον, *to a greater degree, more, rather,* μᾶλλον δέ *'or rather'*, παντὸς μᾶλλον 'more than anything', 'most definitely', 'incontrovertibly' — Sup. μάλιστα, *most of all, more than anyone/ anything, in particular* (τί μάλιστα; 'what exactly/ precisely?'), *in the best way/ best,* in replies *most certainly, absolutely,* with numerals *approximately*

μέντοι[1434]

• Adversative, *and yet, however, but* ~ emphatic *really you know, well let me tell you*
• Often reinforces a personal or demonstrative pronoun which opens the sentence, as σὺ μέντοι, 'you, yes you'

μετα-μέλειν[993]

• *repent:* used impersonally, as μεταμέλει μοι τούτων, literally 'it repents me of this' (ctr. vb μετα-μέλεσθαι, e.g. μετεμέλοντο οὐ δεξάμενοι, 'they regretted the fact that they had not welcomed <it>'); alternatively + dat. and part., as μεταμέλει μοι τοῦτον τὸν κίνδυνον κινδυνεύσαντι, 'I deeply regret having taken/ the fact that I took this risk'

μήν[1436]

• *indeed*, in questions *well now/ then*, τί μήν; an emphatic *of course*
• In statements, *again, further, well* (freq. καὶ μήν 'and what's more')
• Objecting, *no, yet*, οὐ μήν 'certainly not'

μικρός[587]

• *small, litle, insignificant, trivial, petty*
• μικρόν adverbial = *a little*, also σμικρῷ + Comp..
• μικροῦ δεῖν[1210] or μικροῦ alone = *almost, virtually*, cf. s. adj. ὀλίγος[520]

μιμνῄσκεσθαι[1120]

• In aor. *mention:* + περί and gen., or gen. alone
• In perf., *remember, recall*, + gen., or (gen. +) part., as ἆρα μέμνησαι ἀπελθών; 'do you remember that you went away?', μέμνημαί σου μαχεσαμένου αὐτῷ, 'I recall that you fought with him'

νέος[590]

• *young, youthful* (οἱ νεώτεροι as opposed to οἱ πρεσβύτεροι *(the) young(er) men, the young set*), *new*; also *novel, untoward* (so too in Comp., as νεώτερόν τι ποιεῖν, 'do something too innovatory/ pretty startling' by, for instance, taking unexpectedly harsh measures, or engaging in subversive activities; cf. vb νεωτερίζειν[997])

νοῦς[127]

• Common is τὸν νοῦν [but τὸν νοῦν is sts suppressed] προσέχειν 'direct one's attention to', + dat.
• Also *sense, intelligence*, often νοῦν ἔχειν, and
• *purpose*, ἐν νῷ ἔχειν 'have it in mind' to do, + fut. inf.

ὁ[1440]

• Frequently serves as demonstrative pronoun, e.g. ὁ δέ 'and/ but he', ὁ μὲν ... ὁ δέ 'the one ... the other', τῇ μὲν ... τῇ δέ 'on one side ... on the other', 'partly ... partly', πρὸ τοῦ 'before this point'

οἷος[1444]

• *the kind of person who/ thing which* (often conjoined with τοιοῦτος, as εἵλεσθε τοῦτον, ὄντα τοιοῦτον οἷός ἐστιν, 'you elected this individual — a man of his sort!', cf. (τοιοῦτος) οἷος + inf., 'the sort of person to ...'); in indirect questions, *what kind of,* etc. (as e.g. ἐπιχειρῶμεν εὑρεῖν οἷόν ἐστι δικαιοσύνη, 'let us attempt to discover what sort of thing justice is/ the nature of justice')

• In exclamations, οἷον εἰργάσασθε, 'what a thing to have done!'

• οἷον adverbially *for example*

• οἷα + part. like ἅτε, *naturally, since* or *given that*

• Note also:

οἷός (-α -όν) τε [τε a generalising particle] used predicatively with 'be', 'prove' (expressed or understood), *possible, able* (to, inf.), as οἷός τ᾽ ἐστὶ τὰ χρήματ᾽ ἀναλίσκειν, 'he's capable of spending the money', οὐχ οἷόν τε, '<it's> not practicable'

ὀλίγος[520]

• *little, small* : ὀλίγῳ or adverbial ὀλίγον with comparatives, *a little, slightly* more ...

• ὀλίγου δεῖν or ὀλίγου alone *almost, virtually,* cf. s. μικρός[587]

• Plur. *few* (οἱ ὀλίγοι *oligarchical party, oligarchy)*

ὅλος[521]

• *whole, complete, entire*

• 'the whole of' is expressed by ὅλος + article (or article + ὅλος) + noun, as δι' ὅλης τῆς νυκτός, 'through the whole of the night', τὸ ὅλον πρόσωπον, 'his entire face'

• Adv. ὅλως *altogether, in general* or *in short,* οὐχ ὅλως *not at all*

ὅπως[1453]

• [direct form πῶς] *in what way, how* (often with fut. indic. to express object of endeavour, as πράττειν ὅπως ... 'take steps to ensure that ...'; also in elliptical constructions, e.g. ὅπως ταῦτα μηδεὶς πεύσεται, '<just see to it> how (i.e. that) nobody gets wind of this!')

• *in order that*

• οὐχ ὅπως ... ἀλλὰ καί *not only ... not ... but also/ actually* ὅς[1454]

• *who, which, that,* sts bearing a causal sense, *in that/ seeing that he* etc.
• Also serves as sentence-connective, e.g. ἃ ἰδόντες ἔφυγον, 'upon seeing this they ran away', ἀνθ᾽ ὧν 'for these reasons/ this reason', etc.
• εἰσὶν οἵ "some people", ἔστιν ἅ 'some things/ elements' etc.
— Cf. also s. φάναι[1371]

ὅσος[1455]

• *as much/ far/ long/ many as,* (plur.) *all who/ everything that; how much* etc.
• ὅσον οὐ *all but* cf. μόνον[518] οὐ; ὅσον or ὅσον μόνον *only*
• ὅσῳ ... τοσούτῳ + Comp., *the more ... the more ...*

ὅστις[1456]

• *whoever/ whatever, one/ a person who* etc.; in neut. ὅτι *that* (commonly prefaces *direct* speech as well as indirect), *in what way/ how, to what extent, why*
• In neut.. sing. + Sup., = ὡς, as ὅτι τάχιστα
• ὅτι μή (after a neg. clause) *except*

οὗτος[1468]

• *this, that,* often *this/ that particular ...,* sts *the latter*
• Also emphatic 3rd person pronoun, *he* etc.
• τοῦτο μέν ... τοῦτο δέ a formal 'on the one hand ... on the other hand', 'firstly ... secondly'
• καὶ ταῦτα *and that, too/ and ... at that*
• ταύτῃ *in this way/ respect, on this principle*
• ἐν τούτῳ *at this juncture* or *meanwhile*

πάλαι[828]

• *a long time ago,* or *a while* [not necessarily a long while] *ago*
• Commonly with pres. tense in past sense, πάλαι θαυμάζω 'I've long been marvelling'

παρεῖναι[1364]

• *be present, on the spot, here/ there;* τὰ παρόντα *the current situation,* ἐν τῷ παρόντι *at the present moment, in the present (critical) situation*
• Impers., + dat. and inf., *it is possible for/ open to*

παρ-έχειν[1011]

• *provide, furnish, offer, cause* (cf. s. n. ὄχλος, πρᾶγμα)
• With predicate, βελτίους αὐτοὺς παρέχω, 'I make them better', + reflexive, σώφρονα παρέσχεν αὐτόν, 'he showed himself to be restrained'

• Impers., + dat. and inf., *it is in the power* of one to do
• In middle, *adduce, bring forward* evidence, witnesses

πάσχειν[1013]
• *have happen to one* (often euphemistically π. τι, cf. our 'if something should happen to me'), *experience, undergo, suffer,* as εὖ πάσχεις, 'you are being well treated', βίαια ἔπαθον, 'I was subjected to violent treatment'
• Often with adv. + ὑπό and gen., *be treated* in a certain way by one

ποιεῖν[1266]
• *make, do, cause, create, compose;* with personal acc., *do to, treat,* as εὖ ποιεῖν τὸν ἐχθρόν, 'to treat one's enemy well', τὴν πόλιν ἀγαθὰ ποιεῖν, 'to benefit one's country'
• Middle, *count, reckon, consider as ...,* as περὶ πολλοῦ ποιεῖσθαι, 'to value highly, greatly appreciate'; also periphrastically with nouns of action, e.g. διδασκαλίαν ποιεῖσθαι = διδάσκειν[911]

ποῖος[1477]
• *what sort of?* (occasionally in indirect questions)
• Also commonly used in conjunction with a word repeated from the previous speaker's sentence, in an indignant, irritated, incredulous reply, like our 'What do you mean x?!': Χαρμίδου τάδ' ἐστί — ποίου Χαρμίδου;

πολύς[718]
• *much* (πολύ or πολλῷ + Comp. *much, far more...*), *ample, abundant, long*
• Plur. *many, numerous,* οἱ πολλοί *the greater number, the people, ordinary people,* cf. ὡς ἐπὶ τὸ πολύ *for the most part, usually,* τὰ πολλά *in the main,* etc.
• Linked to another adj. by καί, πολλὰ κἀγαθά 'many blessings'

ποτε[1480]
• *at some time, ever, once upon a time*
• *in due course, eventually,* as e.g. ἐπειδή[1421] ποτε
• In questions, τί ποτ' ἐστὶ τοῦτο; 'whatever is this?', 'what can this possibly be?'

πότερος[1481]
• *which of the two,* in direct or indirect questions
• Note in particular adverbial πότερον ... ἤ, as πότερον ὁμολογεῖς οὕτως ἤ οὔ; 'do you agree with this or not?' (πότερον sts prefaces a question with no alternative expressed)
• Also used in the sense *one or other, either of the two*

πράττειν[1023]

• *carry out* (πολλὰ πράττειν 'be a(n interfering) busybody'), *execute, be engaged in, manage, negotiate;* + dat. person, *act* on someone's behalf, be his agent
• *fare*, as εὖ πράττομεν, 'we're doing well'
• In active or middle, with double acc., *exact* payment *from* one

πρός[847]

• + acc., *towards, against, in respect of, touching, in comparison with, relative to, in view of, in the light of*
• + gen., *on the side of, towards, in one's favour,* (swear etc.) *by/ in the name of*
• + dat. *near, at, off, in addition to*
• Without case, *besides,* e.g. καὶ πρός 'and in addition/ on top of that'

προσήκειν[1028]

• Impers., + dat. and inf., *be appropriate, proper,* also τὸ προσῆκον *what is proper, propriety,* τὰ προσήκοντα *approprate conduct, one's duties*
• *be related,* οἱ προσήκοντες *relations*

πῶς[1484]

• *how?,* also *how come?*
• Often πῶς οὐ ...; 'how not ...?' i.e. 'surely ...', as πῶς οὐ δίκαιός ἐστ' ἀπολωλέναι; 'surely he deserves to die!' — In reply πῶς γὰρ/ δ' οὔ; 'why/ but of course', 'that must be so'

ῥάδιος[603]

• Adv. ῥαδίως [cf. ῥᾳθύμως] often *with equanimity* (as ῥαδίως φέρειν a setback etc.], *lightly, casually, carelessly, recklessly*

σπουδή[322]

• *hot haste, exertion* (σπουδὴν ποιεῖσθαι 'exert oneself'), *determined effort*
• Also *seriousness, serious pursuit/ question*
• σπουδῇ *in haste, busily;* or *seriously, earnestly* (as σπουδῇ ἀκούειν)

συμβαίνειν[1042]

• *correspond, fit*
• *agree, come to terms* (with: dat.)
• *happen, come about:* often used impers., + acc./ dat. and inf., as συνέβη τὴν γυναῖκα ἁμαρτεῖν τῆς ὁδοῦ, 'it so happened that the woman lost her way'; τὸ συμβεβηκός, τὰ συμβεβηκότα *event(s), accident(s), occurrence(s)*

ταχύς[706]
- Neut. ταχύ commonly for ταχέως
- Comp. θᾶττον often *pretty quickly, double quick;* ἐπειδὴ θᾶττον or *more often*
Sup. ἐπειδὴ τάχιστα *as soon as, the moment that*

τελευτᾶν[1163]
- *bring to completion, accomplish,* with or without τὸν βίον *die*
- *come to an end:* often personally in part., e.g. τελευτῶντες ἐπόλεμησαν, 'they eventually went/ ended up going to war'

τέλος[451]
- Also: *power of decision, office* (οἱ ἐν τέλει *those in authority*), hence τὰ τέλη (*government) officials, magistrates*
- *military unit, squadron*
- (plur.) *payment, expenditure, taxes paid*
- τέλος also adverbially, *at last, finally*

τιθέναι[1370]
- *put, place, render,* (active or middle) *regard* (... as) or *posit,* with ἐν + dat. *put in the category of, classify as*
- *make, enact* (in middle, *pass) a law*
- In middle, *arrange, manage, dispose*

τις[1491]
- Postp., *some(one), some(thing)* etc., *a (certain),* sts *somebody of note* (δοκοῦσί τινες εἶναι διὰ τὴν εὐπορίαν, 'their affluence gives them a reputation for being important people', cf. λέγειν τι, 'say something <meaningful>', 'talk sense'), *some considerable* ...(as e.g. μέρος τι, 'to a significant extent', 'largely'), *some degree of* ...; neut. also *to some extent* (commonly καί τι καὶ ..., 'and to some degree [etc.] also ...'), *in any respect* etc.
- With adj. *kind of,* as ἄδικός τις εἶ, 'you're a dishonest sort of chap'

τυγχάνειν[1057]
- *hit the mark, succeed,* + gen. *hit* (opp.: ἁμαρτάνειν), *meet with, come upon, obtain, be granted*
- Combined with part. to express *happen to* or *actually,* as ἔτυχον στρατευόμενοι, 'they happened to be engaged in military operations', τυγχάνει ἰατρὸς ὤν, 'he is a doctor in actual fact'

99

ὕβρις[362]

• = *outrageous* (excessive/ uncontrolled/ self-indulgent) *behaviour* (or the state of mind that engenders such behaviour, *unbridled insolence*) inflicting humiliation on another, in the form of physical violence and/ or verbal insult

ὑπό[861]

• + acc., *under, to a point underneath/ under cover of, under the control of, at/ about the time of*
• + gen., *from under, beneath, by/ at the hands of/ through the agency of, as a result of*
• + dat., *under, at the foot of, under the control of, subject to*

φάναι[1371]

• *say*, + (acc. and) inf. (οὐ φ. 'say that ... not')
• *say so, say yes*, as φαμὲν ἢ οὔ; — φαμέν, '[Do we say] Yes or no?' — 'Yes'
• Note also ἦν'I said', ἦ 'he/ she said', from a vb ἠμί 'I say' whose other parts are rare in prose; esp. common are the formulae ἦν δ' ἐγώ '(and) I said', ἦ δ' ὅς/ ἤ '(and) he/ she said' (also ἦ δ' ὃς ὁ Γλαύκων '(and) Glaucon said')

φιλότιμος[665]

• *loving/ aspiring to honour*, whether selfishly *ambitious* or (by performing services to the community and gaining distinction [τιμή[331]] from that) *public-spirited, patriotic*

φρονεῖν[1286]

• *think* in a certain way (τὰ τῶν Λακεδαιμονίων φρονεῖν i.e. sympathise with them, support them):
• εὖ φρονεῖν 'be in one's right mind' (φρονεῖν alone often = *possess understanding, be prudent/ intelligent*), μέγα φρονεῖν 'be presumptuous, big-headed/ ambitious' (+ ἐπί and dat. 'take pride in', as μέγα φρονοῦμεν ἐπὶ τῇ οἰκίᾳ)

χάρις[383]

• Note common expression χάριν εἰδέναι + dat., 'be grateful' to one (also χάριν ἔχειν)
• χάριν + gen. *on account of, for the sake of*, σὴν χάριν 'in order to please you', 'for your sake'

χρῆσθαι[1179]
- *use,* often *treat* (commonly + acc. of respect, as ὅτι ἂν βούληται χρῆται αὐτῇ, 'he treats her as he likes'), *deal/ associate with*
- Also often *experience, encounter* (e.g. νόσῳ, συμφορᾷ)

ὡς[1498]
- As conj., *that/ to the effect that, since/ because/ given that, when/ after, (according) as*
- As adv., *how!,* (+ Sup. adj. or adv.) *as ... as possible* (also reinforces positive adv., as ὡς ἀληθῶς, 'in a true sense', 'really and truly'), (with numerals) *about,* (with part.) *on the ground that, on the pretext of, in the belief that, under the impression that,* (with fut. part.) *with the intention of,* (restrictively) *for,* as in the Sophoclean (you have gone) μακρὰν .. ὡς γέροντι .. ὁδόν, 'a long way for an old man', similarly with inf., as ὡς ἔπος εἰπεῖν, 'so to speak' = 'just about', 'virtually', 'all but'
- As prep., *to* (a person/ person's house/ place etc.), *to join*

INDEX

INDEX

109

INDEX

111

CPSIA information can be obtained
at www.ICGtesting.com
Printed in the USA
LVHW032344280119
605608LV00008B/297/P